THE WASHINGTON, DC.,

ETHNIC

RESTAURANT GUIDE

YOUR PASSPORT TO GREAT ETHNIC DINING

D1564824

ABOUT THE AUTHOR

Jonathan Stein has lived in Washington, DC., since 1979 where he attended graduate school at Georgetown University's School of Foreign Service. He has worked in a foreign policy think tank, where he thought mostly about where to eat. When he's not experimenting with new ethnic recipes or reviewing new restaurants, he works on the staff of the Senate Foreign Relations Committee.

ACKNOWLEDGMENTS

MANY THANKS to all those who suggested their favorite restaurants and who ceaselessly offered their input and suggestions, even after I begged them in the name of all that was holy to please stop!

But seriously, I would like to thank - using Senate parlance, if I might - my good friends and esteemed colleagues who have contributed their time and taste buds to this project: first, my wife and foremost critic (uh, that is, food critic) Betty Borden, quickly followed by Dennis Culkin, Ken and Anne Luongo, Randy DeValk, Mary Savino, Jon Thoren, Fairley Spillman, Cheri Wiggs and Rich Monastursky, Ed Salazar and Anita Friedt, Drew Onufer, Ann Atkins Wright, Dan Stein/Tom Rosenbaum/Steve Seibner (a.k.a. the Brotherhood), John Long and Bruce MacDougal, Joyce Silberstang and Peter Means, Fast Edwin, Rachel and Mike Lostumbo, Isabella Cascarano and Chris Cassel, and Avery Cardoza.

THE WASHINGTON, DC.,
ETHNIC
RESTAURANT GUIDE

YOUR PASSPORT TO GREAT ETHNIC DINING

JONATHAN STEIN

OPEN ROAD PUBLISHING

**To Betty**

1st Edition

Library of Congress Catalog Card No. 93-85359
ISBN 1-883323-01-0

Front cover photo courtesy of Duangrats Restaurant.
Illustrations by Goldstein/Masterson, Portland, Oregon.

CONTENTS

INTRODUCTION

Ethnic dining has exploded in the United States! Nowhere is this trend more pronounced than in Washington, DC and environs. In the last ten years or so, hundreds of ethnic restaurants have opened in the nation's capital, representing an enormous variety of cuisines from every part of the globe. In this book, you'll find the first comprehensive guide to the best ethnic restaurants in the Washington area.

I've included cuisines from more than 30 countries and regions, covering more than 125 ethnic restaurants in the District, northern Virginia, and suburban Maryland. You'll get my top twenty picks, the best places for value, as well as the best dishes to order in each restaurant and those dishes to stay away from. You'll also find a general index and an index arranged by location.

I have been to every place reviewed here several times or more. None of the restaurants knew that I was reviewing them, my thought being that if I announced my presence, the meal served would have been given those special touches and that extra preparation that the dining public would not ordinarily receive. I think the book better serves you and is a much better product than it otherwise would have been for this reason.

By definition, this guide is opinionated. If a dish doesn't quite measure up in one of these fine establishments, I let you know. My standard has been ethnic restaurants that are either very good, great, or out of this world, regardless of price. Please also bear in mind that it's conceivable I will have left out some of your favorite places, but my hope is that you 'll be introduced to a wide variety of fun and interesting restaurants, representing exotic and delicious foods from around the world.

Now go out there and explore a new ethnic restaurant!

AUTHOR'S PREFACE

When I moved to Washington in the summer of 1979, my excitement at attending grad school in foreign policy studies in the nation's capital was outstripped by one thing only: my confident expectation that I would finally live in a city absolutely hopping with a large variety of great ethnic restaurants - the better to understand all those foreign peoples my professors told me I should get to know. My mind and my taste buds reeled in post-collegiate anticipation. If the military's motto was join the Navy and see the world, mine was explore foreign cultures and eat their tasty food.

Imagine the shock to my culinary and ethnologic sensibilities when I discovered that there were, in fact, precious few truly great ethnic eateries in this burg. There were a handful of fine ethnic restaurants, and a number of okay places, but the number and scope were far more limited than I thought possible in a city that has been home to tons of foreign embassies for nearly two hundred years.

But all that changed during the early 1980's. Mostly owing to a growing migration of Asian, Latin American, African, and Middle Eastern emigrés to this area, there has been an explosion of good, great, and fantastic ethnic restaurants in the District, Northern Virginia, and suburban Maryland. The tired, poor, huddled masses have been coming to the Washington area in great droves and opening up everything from simple food stalls to fancy dining establishments. San Francisco, New York, and L.A. may still have a larger number and greater variety of ethnic food joints, but Washington now indisputably ranks as one of the great ethnic restaurant towns in the United States - happily so for resident lovers of exotic and delicious cuisines.

WHAT IS ETHNIC CUISINE IN THE 1990'S?

Good question! Ethnic food is broadly defined here as any cuisine that hails from a distant clime <u>and</u> has not yet fully entered the mainstream American palate. Ethnic food is also at least <u>somewhat</u> exotic and unusual, although this is obviously in the eye (or more accurately the *mouth*) of the beholder. This definition implies a growing number of close calls, because ethnic grub is increasingly favored by more Americans, and is becoming less strange and more accessible.

Italian, Mexican, and Chinese food are particularly well known and well liked now, and are no longer considered offbeat choices. But it would be bizarre to exclude them simply because they are no longer alien to us: these cuisines are still definitely ethnic.

On the other hand, despite their foreign origins, French and most Continental foods are out, as are steak places, seafood houses, delis, and so on. When I talked to friends about this book, classifying Italian food presented the most debate. Jeff Smith, TV's Frugal Gourmet, put out his popular Immigrant Ancestors cookbook a few years back and included recipes from 35 immigrant groups - but not, interestingly, Italian.

No criticism intended, because a writer has to make choices and cannot always include everything. A good case can, in fact, be made to exclude Italian restaurants from this book too, on the grounds that Italian food has become so thoroughly American that it hardly qualifies anymore as a different or unusual cuisine. But as I noted above, Italian (one of our oldest ethnic restaurant groups) is included here in the name of inclusiveness, and I have gone out of my way to find a limited number of great Italian places that offer both Old World-style and nouveau specialties.

I would have liked to include some additional cuisines, particularly East European and Russian, but the sad fact is that the few area restaurants representing our new friends from the old Soviet bloc need to take some lessons from their brethren in New York, where some fantastic Russian, Ukrainian, Polish, and Hungarian places have been serving great food fro a long time. And it would be nice to have a few ethnic restaurants serving up delicious specialties from places like Tibet, Armenia, the Central Asian republics, and other exotic locales.

There you have it! I welcome your input and advice, so please write me with suggestions, comments, and updates. Remember, restaurants often come and go, so call first to make sure one of the dynamite places I've recommended in here is still alive and well. I look forward to hearing from you.

Jonathan Stein

PRICE KEY

The categories I've used for pricing are fairly broad. I've talked to people who consider $15 a lot for a meal, and others who think $35 a person is reasonable. Go figure. So here are my price ranges for the three categories I've used throughout the book. I've included the price of a soft drink, but not a mixed drink, so add a few bucks more if you're going to order wine, beer, or a mixed drink. Tax and tip are excluded as well.

Inexpensive: Less than $15.
Moderate: $15-30.
Expensive: $30 and up.

On those few close calls where the price is borderline, I've listed it as a range, for example, MODERATE-TO-EXPENSIVE.

CREDIT CARD KEY

AE = American Express
C B= Carte Blanche
DC = Diners Club
DV = Discover
MC = MasterCard
V = Visa

OTHER USAGE

Each restaurant reviewed includes information you need to get going. You'll find the address, followed by the phone number, nearest metro (if none is within walking distance, you'll see "N/A" - not available), hours, credit cards accepted, and price.

Other than the credit card key listed on the previous page, I saw no reason to throw in a bunch of symbols, shorthand, or pictographs describing quality, value, ambiance, or other sundries. Better to say it in English than express it through logarithmic functions.

"Daily" next to the hours means open seven days a week.

A Note On Spelling: I've followed the usage of the restaurant in each case, so you'll find dishes spelled differently between restaurants, including punctuation marks, which often differ from place to place within the same ethnic category.

THE TOP TWENTY

Bacchus - Lebanese
Bamiyan II - Afghani
Bangkok Vientiane - Laotian/Thai
Bombay Palace - Indian
Café Atlantico - Caribbean
Crystal Thai - Thai
Duangrat's - Thai
Galileo - Italian
Grill from Ipanema - Brazilian
Hisago - Japanese
Makoto - Japanese
Meskerem - Ethiopian
Primi Piatti - Italian
RT's - Cajun/Creole
Saigonnais - Vietnamese
Sarinah Satay House - Indonesian
Straits of Malaya - Malaysian
Taberna del Alabardero - Spanish
Tony Cheng's Mongolian Restaurant - Chinese/Mongolian
Woo Lae Oak - Korean

AFRICAN

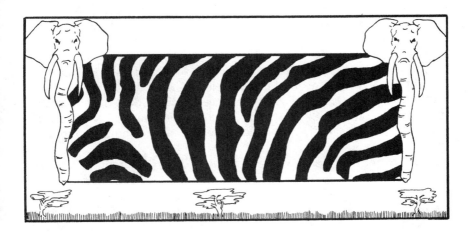

BEAU GESTE

1805 18th St., NW, Washington, DC (202/986-6540). **Nearest Metro:** Dupont Circle on the Red Line. **Hours:** Sun-Th, 5:30 pm - 1:00 am; Sat.-Sun., 5:30 pm - 3:00 pm. **Credit Cards:** AE, CB, DC, MC, V. **Price:** MODERATE.

Beau Geste may conjure up images of Gary Cooper and the French Foreign Legion fighting the infidels in some parched corner of the Sahara, but this Beau Geste is a much nicer watering hole. The food is West African, a region not noted for overly spicy cuisine. The decor is simple, with African wood carvings and a few paintings. If you want to sit on the floor (on cushions), ask for the "Marrakesh" room on the second floor.

For appetizers, I found the **Crabe Farci** (lightly baked crab meat) all right but not too exciting. It would be improved if the crab shell fragments were missing in action. Try the **Meat Pastel** instead, a simple but tasty beef pastry dish, which comes with a pleasing onion dipping sauce. Or start with **Dialdially**, a salad made with mango (or papaya, depending on the season) and avocado.

The entrée selection is rather small, but does fairly represent a nice sampling of foods from West Africa. Try the **Yassa**, grilled marinated lamb or chicken, cooked in a lemon-flavored onion sauce. For something a little heartier, try the **Sauce Feuille**, crabs, shrimp, beef, and lamb stewed in spinach and flavored with palm oil. The **Maffe** is another winner, beef and lamb cubes cooked in a peanut sauce (not quite like the Indonesian or Malaysian *satay* sauce you may know) with your choice of assorted vegetables or okra. If you're a seafood fan, there are several interesting choices, but I'd go with the **Tieboudieune**: grouper and vegetables served on a bed of rice. And if you call a day in advance and have a party of at least four, try the **Matatou** (Basmati rice cooked in a chicken and seafood stew) or the **Mechoui** (Couscous topped with baked lamb).

The side dishes may take some getting used to: the **Banana Foutou**, mashed bananas molded into a small circle, is a very doughy glop that frankly doesn't taste like much, but I'm told it's pretty authentic. The **Plantains**, fried bananas, are more to my liking. There's also a nice variety of fresh fruit drinks, including **Soursop** (made from a white berry) and **Guava Juice.**

The word Terranga appears on the front cover of your menu. It means "welcome" in Ouolof, a Senegalese tribal language. The folks at *Beau Geste* lay out a warm *terranga* for you, so accept their hospitality and try something new!

FASIKA'S

2447 18th St., NW, Washington, DC (202/797-7673). **Nearest Metro:** Dupont Circle on the Red Line. **Hours:** M-Th, 5:00 pm - 1:00 am, sometimes later; F-Sun., 5:00 pm - 3:00 am. **Credit Cards:** AE, CB, DC, DV, MC, V. **Price:** MODERATE.

There are still some decent Ethiopian places from the old days - Red Sea, for example - but precious few that make it beyond the merely adequate. **Fasika's** goes beyond the ordinary and presents excellent food with dash and style. You can choose to have the food placed on a tray sitting on a basket, and eat with your hands with *injera* (the chewy soft bread used for scooping your food) or eat Western-style. At Fasika's, more of the dishes lend themselves to both styles, so I'll describe dishes here as if you're going to order them solo - and you decide how to eat them!

Appetizers are exceptional here. Start with the **Sambusa**, a pastry shell stuffed with lentils, onions, green peppers, and herbs; it's got more of a kick than others I've tried. Another winner is the **Buticha**, a chick pea dip mixed with garlic, olive oil, onions, and lemon juice, perfect for dipping your *injera* bread.

Fish and seafood selections are first rate; try the **Shrimp Tibs**, shrimp marinated in Ethiopian honey wine, rosemary, and *awaze* sauce (honey wine, garlic, onions, and berbere sauce) or, if you're really hungry, the **Seafood Combo** (shrimp, fish, and scallops, cooked in Ethiopian herbs and spices). If you prefer a vegetarian dish, there are several good ones; I like the **Kik Wat** (split yellow peas cooked in red pepper sauce) and the **Kinchem**, an Ethiopian-style couscous.

For beef, I like the **Gomen Be Sega**, a sautéed beef dish with collard greens, onions, peppers, peppercorns, and spiced with cardamom; the **Zilzil**, lamb leg slices marinated in that great *awaze* sauce, then fried in butter; the **Doro Wat**, lemon chicken in red pepper sauce seasoned with garlic, onions, ginger and fenugreek; and, for something hot and spicy, the **Lem Lem Wat**, chopped prime beef cooked in Ethiopian spices and herbs.

Don't forget the weekend nightclub acts, which stay on 'till the wee hours. But whenever you come to **Fasika's**, you'll be treated to some excellent food from the Horn of Africa.

MESKEREM

2434 18th St., NW, Washington, DC (202/462-4100). *Nearest Metro:* Dupont Circle on the Red Line. *Hours:* M-Th, Noon-Midnight; F-Sun., Noon - 1:00 am). *Credit Cards:* AE, CB, DC, MC, V. *Price:* MODERATE.

Meskerem gets my vote for the all-around best Ethiopian place in town, besting its competitors up and down 18th St. in Adams Morgan by a safe distance - although Fasika's across the street is very good too. There are many Ethiopian (and increasingly Eritrean) restaurants in the area, but most of them fall flat much of the time. *Meskerem* is consistently praiseworthy.

You can eat downstairs in a Western-style dining room, or upstairs in traditional Ethiopian style, where you'll sit on cushions on the floor and eat with your hands; your food is served on a round gold-plated tray set atop a basket. If your knees won't give out, upstairs is more fun and authentic. And on weekend nights, live acts entertain with Ethiopian music.

The **Sambusa** are shells stuffed with vegetables and herbs; each Ethiopian place seems to make it a little different, but this rendition is one of the best. You can also get a lively unshelled **Spiced Shrimp** in hot sauce appetizer that could use more heat, but is tasty nonetheless.

For the main course, the thing to do is order a variety of meats and seafood, and use the *injera* bread to scoop up the meats, sauces, and blended vegetables (like delicately-spiced lentils, cabbage, collard greens, and potatoes) that come on the side. Any of the chicken, beef, lamb, and shrimp choices are first-rate here. The **tibs** dishes, either shrimp, lamb, or beef are out of this world; they're marinated in wine, onions, peppers, and herbs. If you prefer going the vegetarian route, try the **Yemisir Watt**, lentils in a hot sauce, or the **Tikil Gomen**, with cabbage, carrots, and potatoes.

Almost anything you order here will be well-prepared and nicely seasoned, so follow your instincts and experiment. If you haven't tried Ethiopian food before and would like to give it a whirl, start with *Meskerem*.

ASIAN

BURMA RESTAURANT

740 Sixth St., NW, Washington, DC (202/393-3453). *Nearest Metro:* Gallery Place on the Red Line. *Hours:* Daily, 11:00 am - 3:00 pm, 6:00 pm - 10:00 pm. *Credit Cards:* None. *Price:* INEXPENSIVE.

Burmese food is still alien to those who have ventured forth over the years into exotic Asian cuisines, but there's really no reason that it should be. Curries are big in Burma as they are elsewhere in Southeast Asia, as are the standard ingredients, spices, and herbs like turmeric, tamarind, fish paste, and lemon juice, but the food has a distinctive and wonderful flavor all its own. The blazing spicy heat that is found in many Thai dishes are largely (but not entirely) absent in Burmese cooking.

Set in a small second floor walk-up in Chinatown, *Burma Restaurant* is our only Burmese eatery in town, opened in the mid-1980's by a former Burmese diplomat. For appetizers, the **Spring Rolls** didn't excite me, but the **Golden Fried Prawns** and **Cabbage Rolls** did. The former are served with a sweet and sour chili sauce; the latter are pork wrapped in cabbage leaf, sautéed with tomato, onion, and garlic sauce. The salads are interesting too; my favorite is the **Pickled Green Tea Leaf Salad**, which is made with pickled Burmese green tea leaves, tossed with sesame seeds, garlic, ground shrimp, ground peanuts, lemon juice and other spices. It's delicious, and I'll wager you won't find this gracing too many other menus.

The Burmese noodle dishes are steadier than the vegetable dishes, several of which I've found wanting. For noodles, try the **Mohingar**, thin rice noodles, lemon grass, and crisp fried onions in a fish broth, served with lemon, coriander, and red chili pepper, or the spicier **Kaukswe Thoke**, a mixture of noodles, ground shrimp, onions, cilantro, red chili pepper, garlic, and lemon juice. In these and other noodle entrées, the lemon juice and cilantro really bring out the flavor.

Other fine possibilities include **Beef Curry**, marinated beef sautéed in onions, garlic, ginger, and assorted spices, and another unique dish, the **Sour Mustard Plant**, which is pickled mustard leaves, finely chopped and sautéed with your choice of chicken, pork, or shrimp.

So the next time you think that you want Thai or Chinese, think of trying something completely new; consider *Burma Restaurant*.

ANGKOR WAT

6703 Lowell Ave., McLean, VA (703/893-6077). **Nearest Metro:** N/A.
Hours: Lunch, M-Sat., 11:30 am - 2:30 pm; Dinner, M-Th, 5:00 pm - 9:30 pm;
F-Sat, 5:00 pm - 10:00 pm; Sun., 5:00 pm - 9:30 pm. **Credit Cards:** AE, DC,
DV, MC, V. **Price:** MODERATE.

Angkor Wat is a small, storefront Cambodian restaurant that serves consistently good food from the land of the Khmer. Its namesake in Cambodia is very possibly the finest temple architecture in all of Asia, and a worthy exemplar for the owners of this delightful restaurant. The flavors and preparation are authentic and, while occasionally putting in a sub-par performance, for the most part you'll get a scrumptious feast with caring service.

If you're in the right season, start with their jasmine ice tea, a refreshing twist on our use of lemon in tea. The soups are, as the menu warns, a meal in itself; I like the **Somlaw Mchu Kroeung** myself, a spicy soup cooked with crushed peanuts and tamarind sauce, with your choice of chicken, duck, spare ribs, beef, or seafood, served with steamed rice. A delicious cold appetizer is the **Nhoam Moan**, a chicken salad of sorts with green and red peppers, bean sprouts, onions, carrots and celery. The **Brochettes** - chicken, shrimp, beef, or pork - is an excellent hot appetizer choice, grilled on a skewer and cooked with noodles, vegetables, and a spicy hot fish sauce similar to (but hotter than) the Thai *nam pla*.

Now that you're ready for the entrées, you might want to get the **Kuong**, rice paper wrapped around fried vegetables, meat, and rice noodles; the **Cha Kroeung**, a Khmer specialty consisting of mildly spiced beef, chopped peanuts, and green peppers (another house specialty); **Shrimp Curry**, stir-fried shrimp in a red curry sauce; and **Amok Chicken**, another house specialty made with steamed chicken, peanut sauce, and coconut milk. It is a wonderful dish that I keep coming back to, and it never disappoints.

You might also want to consider a hot pot dish they call **Cambodian Fondue**, or **Yao Hawn**, made with seafood, beef, chicken, noodles, and vegetables. It's a nice idea for a larger group, and you can adjust the heat from mild to very hot and spicy - your call.

Washington deserves more Cambodian restaurants, as long as we get chefs that can cook as expertly as the good people at *Angkor Wat*.

THE CAMBODIAN

1727 Wilson Blvd. Arlington, VA (703/522-3832). **Nearest Metro:** Court House on the Orange Line. **Hours:** M-Sat., 11:30 am - 2:30 pm, 5:00 pm - 10:30 pm; closed Sun. **Credit Cards:** AE, DC, MC, V. **Price:** MODERATE.

If you look up when you walk into **The Cambodian**, you'll notice a colorful variety of Chinese umbrellas. That's indicative of the heavy Chinese influence here; while the restaurant offers both "authentic Cambodian and Chinese" cuisine, there are far more Chinese than Khmer dishes. The Chinese selections are fine for the most part, but there are better places to chow down on chow mein. Cambodian selections are much better here.

Start with **Charbroiled Beef on Skewers** (served with a sweet sauce of pickled carrot and papaya) or **Hatha Trungkroeung** (stuffed chicken wings on a bone). The latter, stuffed with pork, is a bit fatty but very tasty. Or go with a soup: my two favorites are **Khtish**, featuring pineapple and spareribs, and **Machu Kroeung**, made with beef, lemon grass, and tamarind. Or you can get the hot pot, **Chnang Phleung**, a melange of assorted vegetables and seafood, but this is a meal in itself and you'll probably want it for the main dish.

For entrées, I like the **Cambodian Seasoned Chicken** (grilled boneless lemon grass chicken) and the **Chicken Ginger** better than the **Chicken Char-Kroeung**, which for many Cambodians would be the obvious choice. The Char-Kroeung is stir-fried chicken with green peppers and onions in a lemon grass sauce; sounds great, but tastes kind of flat. The **Beef Lok Lak**, besides being easier to say, is a better bet; it's flank steak stir-fried with lime juice, served on a plain but serviceable bed of lettuce and onions.

If you want more of an adventure, try the **Cambodian Fondue**. Made for two, the Fondue is a pot of hot broth and a smattering of shrimp, sliced beef, squid, vegetables, and rice noodles. If this sounds like too much food or too much work, let me steer you to the **Pork Ginger** - just a simple little sliced pork dish with julienned ginger root, but the delicate seasoning (featuring the same kind of fish sauce you may know from Thai food, *nam pla*) really brings home the bacon for me. The seafood is quite good here, but the main Cambodian-style entrée is the **Cambodian Special Shrimp**, which is "quick" sautéed large shrimp, marinated in ginger and garlic and served with spring onions. Delicious! While most of the rice and noodle dishes are perfectly fine, they're all Chinese.

This is an enjoyable place; the service is fast and friendly. I only hope they add more Cambodian dishes!

CHARLIE CHIANG'S

5 locations: 4250 Connecticut Ave., NW, Washington (202/966-1916). **Nearest Metro:** Van Ness on the Red Line; 1912 I St., NW, Washington, DC (202/293-6000). **Nearest Metro:** Farragut West on the Blue Line; 4060 S. 28th St., Arlington, VA (Village at Shirlington) (703/671-4900). **Nearest Metro:** N/A.; 660 S. Pickett St., Alexandria, VA (703/751-8888). **Nearest Metro:** King St. on the Blue Line; and 11832 Sunrise Valley Dr., Reston, VA (703/620-9700). **Nearest Metro:** N/A. **For all five - Hours:** M-Th, 11:30 am - 10:00 pm; F-Sun., 11:30 am - 10:30 pm; **Dim Sum** is available on Sundays from 12:00 - 3:00 pm. **Credit Cards:** AE, MC, V. **Price:** MODERATE.

Charlie Chiang's serves consistently good Chinese food - sometimes excellent food - at moderate prices. Their Szechuan chefs, one from Chengdu, are among the best Chinese chefs in Washington, and their special extra menu, which will be more to the liking of those willing to experiment, is one of the few authentic menus in town. I'd encourage you to give it a try.

On the regular menu, the best appetizer are the **Fried Meat Dumplings**, which are excellent. The **Hot & Sour Soup** has been getting hotter over the years, which I applaud!

For beef entrées, try the **Yu-Shion Pork**, a wonderful pork in a sweet brown sauce; **Charlie Chiang's Pork Special**, shredded pork sautéed in hot pepper sauce and topped with broccoli; and the **Beef Szechuan**, a hot beef and vegetable dish. Other winners include the **Bean Curd Home Style (Ma-Po Tofu)**, one of the best in the city; the **Fresh String Beans Szechuan Style** is another spicy favorite. The **Singapore Rice Noodles** are great; they're thin rice noodles cooked in mild spices. If you want something with a little more kick, try the **Lamb of Two Seasons**, sliced leg of lamb, prepared with hot dry peppers, sautéed in sweet red peppers, broccoli, peanuts, and scallions. It's one of the best Chinese lamb dishes you'll find in DC.

Charlie Chiang is an innovative restaurateur who makes sure that his menu is always fresh and exciting and sees to it that the service is always fast and courteous. If you haven't already tried it - particularly the new Szechuan menu - treat yourself soon.

CHINA GOURMET

4711 Montgomery Ln., Bethesda, MD (301/657-4665). **Nearest Metro:** Bethesda on the Red Line. **Hours:** Sun.-Th, 11:00 am - 10:00 pm; F-Sat., 11:00 am - 11:00 pm. **Credit Cards:** AE, MC, V. **Price:** MODERATE.

As a rule, I am not a big fan of Cantonese (South China) cuisine, except *dim sum*. Szechuan and Hunan food get my vote every time, but **China Gourmet's** mix of different styles - including Cantonese — is pulled off with dash and style.

The **Meat Dumplings**, either fried or steamed, are a good place to start, unless you're in the mood for soup, in which case I'd advise for the classic **Wonton Soup** over the not-so-classic **Hot and Sour Soup,** which was all right but a bit too thick for me. The **fried noodles** are very good here, not at all greasy.

Seafood and shrimp courses are China Gourmet's strengths. For lovers of Cantonese, I'd order the **Jumbo Shrimp in Lobster Sauce** or the **Seafood Delight**, featuring shrimp and scallops cooked with snow peas, straw mushrooms, baby corn, and carrots in a light brown sauce. But I'd stay away from the rather bland **Lobster and Chicken Delicacy**.

The Szechuan dishes are surprisingly hot and peppy! The **Shan Fun Beef**, besides sporting a playful name, is basically a hepped-up, moderately spicy Cantonese dish, with stir-fried vegetables and filet mignon. **General Tso's Chicken** has good heat to it, and is a good representative of this ubiquitous dish. And the **Bean Curd Szechuan Style** (*ma-po tofu*, pronounced *dofu* for you aficionados) was out of this world, almost on a par with the best to be had in these environs. The sauce is delicious, the minced pork done just right.

It took some doing, but when I was finally cajoled into eating here, I was glad I did. I think you'll be pleased too.

CITY LIGHTS OF CHINA

1731 Connecticut Avenue, NW, Washington (202/265-6688). **Nearest Metro:** Dupont Circle on the Red Line. **Hours:** Sun.-Th, 11:30 am - 10:30 pm; F-Sat., 11:30 am - 11:00 pm. **Credit Cards:** AE, DC, DV, MC, V. **Price:** INEXPENSIVE.

Ever busy, **City Lights** has become one of Washington's most popular Chinese restaurants; I can't remember the last time I went on a weekend night and didn't have to wait at least 15-20 minutes. All that popularity seems to have had a bit of a downside, in that the cooking and presentation are not what it once was. Still, **City Lights** is much better than the typical Chinese fare in these parts.

The old standby **Hot and Sour Soup** is a good way to start your meal, as is that even older standby, **Wonton Soup**. Good choices for appetizers include the **Pan-Fried Dumplings**, six to an order, or the **Spicy Chinese Cabbage**, cooked in a hot red chili sauce.

For those of you who like **Peking Duck** (interesting how we haven't changed Peking Duck to Beijing Duck!), you've come to the right place; it's sliced at your table and served with scallions, plum sauce, and those moo shi-like pancakes; their **Twice Cooked Duck** and **Duck Strips in Garlic Sauce**, both hot, are beautifully spiced and not too fatty, as duck too often is.

For other entrées, I'd suggest the **Crisp Fried Shredded Beef**, sautéed in a spicy hot pepper and ginger-based sauce, and served with vegetables; the **Kung Pao Chicken**, chicken in a mildly spicy brown sauce cooked with peanuts; and **Ma Po Tofu**, a superior and hotter version of this bean curd and minced pork classic. And for seafood, also done quite well here, I like the **Scallops and Shrimp in Garlic Sauce** and the crispy **Whole Fish in Black Bean Sauce**.

As I indicated above, **City Lights** occasionally lets you down, sometimes in service, sometimes in food quality. But most of the time, the good people at this popular eatery come through, and when they do, you'll be quite pleased with the result.

GOLDEN PALACE

720-724 7th St., NW, Washington, DC (202/783-1225). **Nearest Metro:** Gallery Place on the Red Line. **Hours:** Sun.-M, 11:00 am - 10:00 pm; T-Sat., 11:00 am - Midnight. **Credit Cards:** AE, MC, V. **Price:** INEXPENSIVE.

There is only one reason to go to **Golden Palace**, and that's for the **Dim Sum**. The Cantonese and Hunan dishes are mediocre, and the Szechuan dishes only a bit better. But the daily dim sum offerings make up for whatever's lacking on the rest of the menu, which explains the weekend crowds - especially for Sunday brunch.

The inside of **Golden Palace** is a snapshot frozen in time, with a circa 1960's pre-Szechuan decor and feel, the kind of Chinese place that my family religiously frequented on Sunday nights in my youth. That look is one of the things I miss in the new style Chinese interiors.

So let's focus on the dim sum, which is not a particular food but rather a Southern (Cantonese) creation. It's a series of hot snacks and sweet dishes to be eaten between the late morning and mid-afternoon with Chinese tea. I'm told it means "eating snacks for happiness." The way it unfolds at **Golden Palace** (and most other dim sum-meries) is as follows: waiters/waitresses waft on by your table pushing carts of small dishes, plunking down a tray of this or a bamboo steamer of that, and toting up your tab as the meal progresses. Sounds like fun, huh?

My favorite dim sum choices here are the **Steamed Shrimp Dumpling**; the **Steamed Roast Pork Bun**; the **8 Treasure Sweet Rice Wrapped in Lotus Leaf** (chicken and sausage and various spices wrapped in sticky rice); and the **Bean Curd Roll in Oyster Sauce**. You should also try a selection of sweet pastries, like the **Steamed Lotus Seed Bun** or the **Egg Custard Tart**. And don't forget to keep your tea bowl full; it does add to the experience.

It takes special training to be a dim sum chef. Judging by the number of Chinese patrons in **Golden Palace**, and by my own taste buds, I'd say their training has paid off. I think you'll agree.

RICKY'S RICE BOWL

4865 Cordell Ave., Bethesda, MD (301/652-7423). **Nearest Metro:** Bethesda on the Red Line. **Hours:** M-F, 11:00 am - 10:00 pm; Sat., Noon - 10:00 pm; closed Sun. **Price:** INEXPENSIVE.

This is Asian fast food at its best. The interior has a sort of pink-neon look, but no decor to speak of. **Ricky's Rice Bowl** is quick, cheap, and good.

The **Spicy Egg Drop Soup** was spicy indeed, and had a hint of corn-flavoring. Repeat daily specials are usually very good, but you need to ask them to pour on the heat if you like it that way; a good example of this is the moderately spiced, low-key **Kubla Khan**, a Mongolian beef hot dish. The great Khan, I feel sure, would have insisted on more pizzaz, but this dish and others like it are less greasy and more flavorful than other fast food alternatives.

The **Peanut Chicken** and **Peanut Beef** dishes are excellent, as is the **Chicken Curry Bowl.** It's hard to find less expensive good eats in this part of Bethesda; you can have soup, two regular-size entrées, and two medium cokes for $11 and change. Not a bad deal at all.

SZECHUAN

615 I St., NW, Washington, DC (202/393-0130). **Nearest Metro:** Gallery Place on the Red Line. **Hours:** M-Th, 11:00 am - 11:00 pm; F-Sat., 11:00 am - Midnight; Sun., 11:00 am - 10:00 pm. **Credit Cards:** AE, DC, DV, MC, V. **Price:** MODERATE.

From its Chinatown perch, **Szechuan** has long been one of the steadiest Chinese restaurants in town. While others came and went, this place remained, making unadorned but high-quality Chinese food for all and sundry.

With a big menu, you won't have too much trouble picking out some winners. Start with **Hot and Sour Soup**, still the best around, or try the ungreasy **Fried Meat Dumplings** or the **Bon Bon Chicken**, spicy shredded chicken in a peanut sauce.

For entrées, the noodle dishes are quite good, particularly the **Dan Dan Noodles**, long thin noodles mixed with a spicy chili sauce of garlic, scallions, and soy. The **Sauteed String Beans** with a hot and spicy meat sauce is excellent, as is the **Ma-Bo's Bean Cake**, known elsewhere as *ma-po dofu*; here it comes with minced pork and has a nice kick.

Other entrées to round out a great meal include **Shredded Chicken in Garlic Sauce**, the **Moo Shi Pork** (spelled *moo shu* in many other places, it's shredded vegetables and pork, over which you pour plum sauce and roll it up into one of the pancakes accompanying the dish), any of the shrimp or scallop dishes, which have always proven their mettle, and one of the **Sizzling Rice** dishes (your choice of pork, chicken, shrimp, or assorted seafood).

Szechuan does several things quite well, but hot and spicy is their forte. If you don't want it hot, they'll cool it down for you, but if you prefer the heat, you should wander in and give it a try.

TONY CHENG'S MONGOLIAN RESTAURANT

619 H St., NW, Washington, DC (202/842-8669). **Nearest Metro:** Gallery Place on the Red Line. **Hours:** Sun.-Th, 11:00 am - 11:00 pm; F-Sat., 11:00 am - Midnight. **Credit Cards:** AE, MC, V. **Price:** MODERATE.

Tony Cheng's Mongolian Restaurant is a fun way to spend a night out and get a good meal in the bargain. You pick out your own fixin's, give it to a barbecue chef, who in turn sizzles it up on the big blackened grill in the center of this spacious and elegant - yet very reasonable - restaurant.

The hot pot/barbecue thing began in China after the 13th century Mongol conquest, and has been refined by Chinese throughout China ever since, adding regional variations through the years. The two main choices are a **hot pot** that you cook at your own table, or the **barbecue** described above. Are either of these authentically Mongolian? Not really, but the idea of a hot pot or large barbecue where you add ingredients is. The hot pot dinner begins with a hot pickled cabbage appetizer. Once your broth is boiling, you add sliced vegetables, tofu, thin noodles, chicken, beef, seafood, and whatever else sounds good.

The barbecue dinner seems to be the more popular choice. Arrayed in small bowls around the center grill are various uncooked but sliced meats: chicken, pork, steak, etc.; lots of sliced veggies, like onions, cabbage, scallions, carrots, green peppers, and so on; and a large number of liquid (and some dry) spices, like ginger oil and garlic oil, sesame oil, hot chili oil, sugar, soy sauce, and the like. You pile it all into your very own bowl and hand it to the master chef, who takes your grub and tosses it on the grill. Moments later, you've got a personalized aggregation of either a mild or spicy - your choice - barbecued treat.

I like this place a lot, perhaps because it gives you the chance to play with your own food a bit before you have it wokked by the pro's! A different twist on Chinese cuisine, *Tony Cheng's Mongolian* is my kind of place.

LITTLE QUIAPO

4807 N. First St., Arlington, VA (703/528-3194). *Nearest Metro:* N/A.
Hours: T-Sun., 11:30 am - 9:00 pm; closed Mon. *Credit Cards:* MC, V. *Price:*
INEXPENSIVE.

Located in the Arlington Forest Shopping Center on Rt. 50, *Little Quiapo*
is, frankly, inconsistent, sometimes handing in a good performance, other
times offering merely adequate food. But when it's on, this little storefront
Filipino place is well worth the time if you're looking for something different
than the usual Asian choices.

Start with the **Chicken Sottanghon**, a thin noodle soup with chicken
pieces, or the **Tokwa and Baboy**, a fried tofu and pork appetizer cooked in
a vinegar and onion sauce. It's a little strange at first, but the vinegar works!
The **Lumpia Shanghai** will sound more familiar to you (it's like an egg roll),
but they're not anything special, although the lemon-based hot sauce is
interesting.

The best entrée by far is the **Adobo**, which comes with either pork or
chicken, and is sautéed in soy sauce , lemon juice, vinegar, and mild spices. The
Pork Sinigang is a simple but tasty pork dish cooked with vegetables in a
lemon flavored sauce. The bold among you may wish to try the **Kare Kare**,
an ox tail stew with vegetables cooked in peanut sauce and accompanied with
small salted (overly salty, in my view) shrimp, or the **Lechon Kawale**, a deep-
fried pork belly dish. I like the **Camaron Rebosado** about as much as the
Adobo; it's a deep-fried shrimp dish, covered in a sweet and sour sauce.

Desserts, like **Leche Flan** (a milky flan, or egg custard) and **Halo-Halo**
(mixed preserved tropical fruits with milk and crushed ice), are good but, as
usual with many ethnic eateries, too sweet. If you order the right things at
Little Quiapo, you'll have a unique and fun dinner.

SABANG

2504 Ennalls Ave., Wheaton, MD (301/942-7859). *Nearest Metro:* Wheaton on the Red Line. *Hours:* M-Th, 11:00 am - 10:00 pm, F, 11:00 am - 11:00 pm; Sat., Noon - 11:00 pm, Sun., Noon - 10:00 pm. *Credit Cards:* AE, MC, V. *Price:* MODERATE.

One of the two best Indonesian places in the area, *Sabang* serves up sumptuous feasts in roomy and refined surroundings. There often seems to be a party or special event going on here, and the large room does lend itself to throwing a shindig here. Located near the Wheaton Plaza, *Sabang* offers friendly service and great food.

Start with the **Lumpia**, an Indonesian egg roll that is lighter than its Chinese counterpart, or the **Ayam Lapis Udang**, sliced stir-fried chicken with shrimp. Similar to a Thai soup, the **Soto Sulung** is a nicely seasoned beef soup cooked with coconut milk.

If you do have a large party, you ought to consider the **Rijsttafel**, a Dutch word meaning "rice table," where you can choose from a huge assortment of dishes featuring white or fried rice in several different combinations. For entrées, the *satays* should not be missed; this is, after all, the land that gave us satay (peanut sauce). I especially like the **Sate Manis**, a marinated beef satay served with fried rice. Some of the better chicken and beef dishes include the **Ayam Bekakak**, a boneless chicken cooked in bekakak - hence the name - which is a fantastic sauce made with onions, garlic, fish sauce, lemon grass, hot red chiles, lime leaves, coconut milk and brown sugar; and the **Sambal Goreng Daging Kentang**, a hot beef and potato dish cooked in coconut sauce.

The traditional **Gado-Gado**, steamed vegetables in a satay sauce, is a must-try here. Seafood dishes are remarkable as well; two of my favorites include the **Sambal Goreng Udang Tahu**, a mildly spicy shrimp and tofu in coconut sauce, and the **Ikan Kakap Asem Manis**, a crispy deep-fried whole snapper - but you'll enjoy the other shrimp, fish, and squid specialties here as well.

The chefs clearly put their all into the many possibilities here. If you like Indonesian food, do yourself a favor and discover *Sabang*.

SARINAH SATAY HOUSE

1338 Wisconsin Ave., NW, Washington, DC (202/337-2955). **Nearest Metro:** N/A. **Hours:** T-Sat., Noon - 3:00 pm, 6:00 pm - 10:30 pm; Sun., 6:00 pm - 10:30; closed Mon. **Credit Cards:** AE, DC, MC, V. **Price:** MODERATE.

    Sarinah Satay House in Georgetown serves top-of-the-line Indonesian food in an attractive setting, complete with large plants and a skylight to give you that tropical feel. A number of years ago I had some doubts about **Sarinah Satay**, in part because of laggard service, but my concerns have been dispelled of late with a series of great meals over the past year.

    Before you begin, let me recommend a popular (and very sweet) Indonesian banana liqueur called **Pisang Ambon**. For soup and appetizers, I like the **Sarinah Wedding Soup**, a mild broth made with wontons, glass noodles, and vegetables. The **Shomai** is just an Indonesian version of the Chinese *shumai* (sort of like a dim sum-wrapped wonton with shrimp or crab). It's better at good Chinese restaurants, so I'd order instead the **Lumpia Goreng**, lightly fried spring rolls that are crisp and tasty.

    The **Gado-Gado** is a popular vegetable dish cooked in peanut sauce; try also the **Asinan**, a spicy, sour vegetable dish with cabbage, tofu, and bean sprouts in vinegar and red chili sauce, served cold. The *satays* sparkle here; if you like lamb, chicken, shrimp, and beef, order the **Satay Kombinasi**. Other winners include the **Ayam Panggang Santen**, a mildly spicy grilled chicken in coconut sauce, or the **Ayam Bumbu Rujak**, a hotter version cooked without coconut sauce. The *udang* (shrimp) dishes are generally good; I like the **Udang Belado**, a hot fried shrimp dish in a red chili sauce, but you can order a different *udang* if you prefer something mild.

    You can also get the traditional **Rijsttafel**, a rice table with your choice of 12 different dishes all cooked with rice; if you don't want your whole meal taken over by the rice table, order from the regular menu and for your rice go for the **Nasi/Lomtong Rames**, a great rice dish cooked with chicken, beef satay, green beans, and shrimp chips.

    Desserts, as you might expect, are on the too-sweet side, but the coffee is usually on target. All in all, **Sarinah Satay House** is a nice place to enjoy some unusually good food.

CHA WON
ORIENTAL EXPRESS

11782 Parklawn Dr., Rockville, MD (301/770-5576). **Nearest Metro:** White Flint on the Red Line. **Hours:** Sun.-M, 10:00 am - 10:00 pm; closed T. **Credit Cards:** MC, V. **Price:** MODERATE.

You won't find **Cha Won** easily - it's tucked away in the Parklawn Center not far from White Flint - but this simple, fun Korean eatery is worth the search. Periodically throughout your meal you'll hear some loud thwacking; in the back of the restaurant the cooks are making long strands of noodles (you can watch through the large pane).

Cha Won is not as fancy as some of the other Korean places around town, but the offerings are authentic and some are fantastic. There are no appetizers, but there are three soups; my recommendation is the **Hot Sour Spicy Soup** - it's not that spicy but the curry base is very tasty. What other area restaurants call *Bulgoki* is here called **Chinese Style Bool Ko Ki Rice**, which the help claims is the truly authentic *Bulgoki*. I find it to be more reminiscent of a Chinese dish than a Korean dish, but it is a good choice nonetheless. The **Boneless Roast Chicken with Sweet and Sour Sauce** also has a definite Chinese feel to it, but if you like sweet and sour sauce, you'll love this one.

The noodle dishes are the main thing at **Cha Won**, the clear winners being the **Jang Won Ban Jum Special Noodle** (a seafood dish in a delicious curry sauce) and the **Yang Jang Pi** (an enormous platter of noodles, beef, and vegetables). The **Noodle with Shrimp and Seafood Soup** is a huge bowl of soup, one of the few dishes here made out of long thin noodles. If you're up for seafood soup, it's a solid choice - but not too exciting. Stay away from the **Noodle with Pork and Bean Sauce**, which looks great but is bland beyond belief.

There are a number of expensive seafood, beef, and pork dishes, but they're designed for two or more. For the true connoisseur, there's **Sea Cucumber**, **Abalone**, and **Shark's Fin** dishes, fresh and fortunately lacking in that overly fishy taste.

Cha Won's noodle dishes are the main reason to visit, and if you order a few of them while experimenting with other parts of the menu, you'll have yourself one fine Korean meal.

SAMWOO

1054 Rockville Pike, Rockville, MD (301/424-0495). **Nearest Metro:** N/A.
Hours: M-F, 11:30 am - 11:00 pm; Sat.-Sun., Noon - 11:00 pm. **Credit Cards:**
AE, MC, V. **Price:** MODERATE.

Samwoo is actually a combined Korean-Japanese restaurant, and, while
some of the Japanese dishes are quite good, why go here for Japanese food
when Korean is really their forte?

Samwoo is in one of those oh-so-charming mini-strip malls dotting the
beautiful Rockville landscape, so you have to look for the sign over the place
while you're cruising up (or down) Rockville Pike, but it's well worth it once you
get inside. The ambiance is fine, there's plenty of room, and the food is usually
quite good.

Many of the main courses are do-it yourself jobs at a little cooker on your
table, or you can let the master chefs here go at it for you. I found it more fun
to sizzle my own food. Let me suggest three typical and delicious Korean
entrées, although I really think you can't go wrong here. The **Bulgoki** is a
simple dish of thin sliced beef. All the meat dishes come with one of several
mild dipping sauces that really add flavor to the meat.

If you want something on the hot and spicy side, the **Dak Gui** is boneless
sliced chicken served in a spicy sauce. It is perfectly seasoned and, if you're
a chicken fan, you'll love it! Next, and akin to the Chinese dish of moo shu,
the **Pa Junyo** is a pancake filled with scallion, beef, and shrimp. Eating too
many of these pleasing pancakes can be a heavy experience for your poor
stomach, so ease up! But they are great!

Samwoo is hopefully one of a growing number of area Korean restaurants. I hope that future additions to this wonderful cuisine are as good a value
as this unassuming strip-mall eatery on Rockville Pike.

WOO LAE OAK

1500 S. Joyce St., Arlington, VA (703/521-3706). **Nearest Metro:** Pentagon City on the Blue Line. **Hours:** 11:30 am - 10:30 pm, daily. **Credit Cards:** AE, DC, MC, V. **Price:** MODERATE-TO-EXPENSIVE.

Woo Lae Oak, situated one block from Pentagon City, is housed in a big residential apartment complex of the kind frequently found in the wiles of Arlington and Crystal City. But it's definitely worth ferreting out; **Woo Lae Oak**, part of a chain with branches in Seoul, New York, and LA, is undoubtedly our finest Korean restaurant. You know it's good the minute you see the clientele: three-quarters Korean on most nights.

The menu is extensive, so you'll have to come back several times to savor all the great Korean fare. Start with the **Goki Jun**, grilled meatballs coated with egg and flour, or the **Pindae Ttok**, a large mung-bean pancake of sorts filled with bean sprouts, pickled cabbage, and vegetables, cooked in a delicious seasoning.

Each table comes equipped with a small burner, so that you can grill your own dinner (what could be more fun than playing with your food over an open fire?). **Bul Goki** is perhaps the most popular dish at Korean restaurants in the US. Like Americans, Koreans love beef. Bul Goki is made here with sirloin steak, cut very thin, and marinated with green onions, garlic, sesame oil, black pepper and sugar. The **Daeji Gui**, thinly sliced pork marinated in their hot and spicy "special sauce," is another clear winner.

The **Bibim Bap**, a grilled marinated beef dish with assorted vegetables is also delicious; the strips of beef are topped with fried egg and a side dish of hot bean paste for dipping. Another bibim dish well worth the effort is **Bibim Neng Myun**, a spicy buckwheat noodle dish topped with sliced beef and vegetables. And don't forget to try the spicy **Kim Chee**, the Korean national side dish: pickled and fermented cabbage, turnips, and cucumbers. It's not for the faint of heart.

If you want something really special, call a day ahead of time and order one of the Chef's Specialties, particularly the **Shin Sul Lo** (a hot pot of beef broth, meatballs, fish and vegetables) or the **Modum Yori**, a classic combo platter of whole grilled fish with shrimp, chicken and beef.

If you're still hungry, be forewarned that desserts here are very sweet. My guess is that your first visit to **Woo Lae Oak** won't be your last.

BANGKOK VIENTIANE

926-A West Broad St. (Rt. 7), Falls Church, VA (703/534-0095). *Nearest Metro:* N/A. *Hours:* 11:00 am - 3:00 pm daily, lunch buffet; 5:00 pm - 9:00 pm daily for dinner. *Credit Cards:* AE, DV, MC, V. *Price:* INEXPENSIVE.

Bangkok Vientiane is without a doubt among the very best Thai places on the scene, and is unparalleled as a Laotian joint. Of course, it's the only Laotian eatery, but who cares? The owners are a husband-wife team; he's Thai, she's Laotian, and the result is one great restaurant! This place is pretty close to unbeatable; for value, there's none better.

I'd urge you to choose more heavily from the Lao dishes initially, given that you can get great Thai food all over Washington and this is your one shot at Laotian cuisine. Start with one of the **spring rolls**, either fresh or fried. They're similar in composition and taste to Vietnamese *cha giao*. Don't miss the **Tum Mark Houng**, a spicy cold papaya salad with shrimp, tomato, hot peppers, dried beef and sticky rice. Even hotter is its Thai cousin on the other side of the menu, **Yum Woun Sen**, a combination salad of shrimp, pork, onion, mint, bean thread, hot peppers and scallions. If you want soup, stay with one of the Thai classics; my favorite here is the **Gai Tom Kha** (chicken, galanga root, lemon grass, mushrooms, and coconut milk).

There are a number of excellent vegetarian dishes; go for the **Mixed Vegetable Curry** or, if you prefer a less spicy dish, the **Mixed Vegetables Stir Fried** is great too. To capture the heart and soul of this place, though, I'd heartily recommend the following: **Gai Yang**, which is grilled marinated chicken in a great "special sauce;" **Lab Mou** or **Lab Gai**, the former being pork, the latter chicken, mixed with green beans, hot peppers, mint, parsley and scallions; and **Vientiane Chicken**, a poached chicken dish smothered in a garlic ginger sauce. If you want some beef, try the **Tiger Cried**, which is a grilled beef dish accompanied by "dipping tearing sauce." It's not nearly as hot as advertised. Try also the **Crepe A La Vientiane**, a mixture of shrimp, scallop, chicken, onion, ground peanuts, bean sprouts and scallions.

On the Thai side of the ledger, I'd recommend the pork or chicken **Pud Panang**, which is prepared with hot peppers, red curry paste, and other Thai spices. Chicken, pork, or beef basil are all delicious too. If you want noodles, the standard **Pud Thai** (more commonly known as pad thai) is very good, as is the **Bamee Krob Rad Nar**, crispy egg noodles with your choice of beef, chicken, or pork, surrounded by bamboo shoots and shrimp.

As if all this great food were not enough, there's an extra added bonus: it's extremely reasonable. With such great food featured for such low prices, you'll come back again and again.

APPETIZER PLUS

1117 N. 19th St., Rosslyn, VA (703/525-3171). **Nearest Metro:** Rosslyn on the Blue/Orange Line. **Hours:** M-Th, 11:30 am - 2:00 pm, 5:30 pm - 10:00 pm; F, 11:30 am - 2:00 pm, 5:00 - 10:30 pm; Sat., Noon - 3:00 pm, 5:00 pm - 10:30 pm; Sun., 5:30 - 10:00 pm. **Credit Cards:** AE, MC, V. **Price:** INEXPENSIVE.

Brought to you by the owners of Matuba, a higher-scale, better restaurant with locations in Bethesda and Arlington, **Appetizer Plus** makes it into this Guide in the "unique" category. For where else can you find a good (if not great) reasonably-priced "All You Can Eat Sushi Buffet" for $14.95 ($13.95 for parties of five or more, but they seem to be open to negotiation on this point). The answer is LA or San Francisco, and possibly New York, but certainly nowhere else in DC.

There is only one reason to frequent this joint: sushi, which is fresh and, true to the restaurant's name, appetizing. They will prepare on request any of the 33 sushi dishes on their menu if it's not sitting out on the buffet table. There are some interesting choices that you don't see every day, like their **Bagel Roll**, cream cheese and smoked salmon wrapped in rice. The **Tuna** and **Yellow Tail** are two of the better selections, but again, you can find better sushi elsewhere — just not at this price.

Appetizer Plus also features a small number of cooked Japanese entrées, from **Tempura** to **Teriyaki** to **Tonkatsu**, the latter a breaded, deep-fried pork. The **Miso Soup**, was, to say the least, uninspired. But unlike a lot of other local Japanese places, Appetizer Plus offers four **Donburi** dishes, which are pretty good. Skip the smorgasbord of hot entrées, where you'll find rather plain dishes of **Grilled Tuna**, **Squid**, **Stir-Fried Chicken** and **Fried Gyoza**, which is a mixture of meat and vegetables wrapped in a lightly-fried dough (akin to Chinese potstickers).

If you want a great traditional Japanese meal, there are other fine establsihments to visit. But if you want to consume large quantities of sushi and sashimi, and not refinance your house to pay for it, then come to **Appetizer Plus**.

GINZA RESTAURANT

1009 21st St., NW, Washington, Washington, DC (202/833-1244). **Nearest Metro:** Farragut North on the Red Line. **Hours:** M-F, 11:45 am - 2:30 pm, 5:00 pm - 11:00 pm; Sat., 5:00 pm - 10:30 pm . **Credit Cards:** AE, CB, DC, MC, V. **Price:** MODERATE.

One of DC's finest Japanese restaurants, **Ginza** is too often treated as a lobbyist lunch hangout. It is less expensive than some of the fancier eateries hailing from the Land of the Rising Sun, such as Hisago. And, while not cheap, it is a good value, with consistently fresh sushi and a large selection of great entrées.

To begin with, any of your favorite sushi choices are very good. There is also a better-than-usual selection of hot appetizers, including **Takosu Miso** (Octopus with soy bean sauce) for the brave of heart and an excellent **Yakitori** (prepared here as barbecued chicken with teriyaki sauce).

For entrées, Ginza has a variety of different options, the better of which include a **"Special Zen Course for Vegetarians,"** hot pot dishes, noodle dishes, **Domburi** (meat and/or vegetables cooked with soy and served in a bowl of rice) and **Ochazuke** (a bowl of rice with seaweed and dried fish, with green tea mixed in for good measure). For fans of domburi (sometimes spelled donburi), **Ginza** offers some of the best around.

There are also complete dinners, featuring **Sukiyaki, Teriyaki, Tempura,** and **Ton Katsu** (breaded pork lightly fried), among others. If you like seafood and noodles, try their **Nabeyaki Udon** (noodles with fish cake, shrimp, egg and vegetables in soup) or **Tempura Soba**, buckwheat noodles with shrimp tempura cooked in a hot clear broth.

Considering how expensive Japanese restaurants often are, **Ginza** is a solid choice for a great meal.

HISAGO

3050 K St., NW, Washington Harbor, Washington, DC (202/944-4181). **Nearest Metro:** N/A. **Hours:** M-F, Noon - 2:30 pm, 6:00 pm - 10:30 pm; Sat.-Sun., 6:00 pm - 10:30 pm. **Credit Cards:** AE, DC, MC, V. **Price:** EXPENSIVE.

Hisago is set overlooking the Washington Harbor. You can enjoy an excellent meal at a table, at the sushi bar, or in tatami rooms (*tatamis* are mats that cover the floor in traditional Japanese homes). The food is about as good as it gets, and, even though they have lowered some of their prices, remains fairly expensive. Still, you'll get an outstanding meal served in an elegant atmosphere.

All entrées come with a simple bean sprout salad, Miso Soup, rice, and *oshinko* (pickled vegetables). You can go straight for the **Sushi a la carte** either for an appetizer or as a dinner, or get a set **Sushi** dinner with nine pieces. The truly expensive items are the **Kaiseki** dinners, which you can get with sushi, tempura, beef, seafood, or in a broth, with a lot of courses. They start at $45 and go up to $100 for the **Chef's Special Kaiseki**, which you'll need to order in advance.

But if you choose to forgo the ultra-fancy option of the *kaiseki*, consider ordering the more down-to-earth **Teriyaki Beef Steak**, a grilled New York sirloin with the chef's delicately seasoned teriyaki sauce. Other top choices here are the **Yosenabe**, an entrée for two with mixed seafood and vegetables boiled in a hot pot at your table; and the **Seafood Steak**, which is assorted grilled seafood, served on a heated stone.

If you can persuade one of your lobbyist pals to take you out somewhere, this place would be one of my top picks. But even if you're under the gun by your friends and family who are dying to try a new Japanese restaurant, unless you opt for the *kaiseki* dinners, you won't break the bank by taking them to a fantastic meal at **Hisago**.

MAKOTO

4822 MacArthur Blvd., NW, Washington, DC (202/298-6866). *Nearest Metro:* N/A. *Hours:* M, W-Sun., Noon - 2:00 pm. 6:00 pm - Midnight; closed Tues. *Credit Cards:* MC, V. *Price:* MODERATE-TO-EXPENSIVE.

Makoto is most definitely not a sushi bar - there is no separate sushi section on the menu, although there are a few sushi dishes - but there is a small bar where you can be served and watch the master chef (owner of **Sakura Palace** in Silver Spring) do his thing. The tasteful decor is reminiscent of a small restaurant in Tokyo or Kyoto, with just a few tables. Remove your shoes at the door, and get ready for a fabulous meal.

The dinner menus are preset and will run you about $25. During the evening you'll be treated to mustard-flavored, hot **Watercress;** a tasty *udon/soba* dish featuring buckwheat noodles with seaweed and mushrooms; **Inarizushi,** fried tofu pockets filled with vinegared rice and vegetables; **Futomaki**, a big-roll sushi cut into a number of smaller pieces, sometimes with vegetables, sometimes with different raw fish slices; **Tsukuri** (cooked tuna) and **Toro**, a fancier version of tsukuri; **Yakitori,** broiled and braised chicken; **Yakimono** (the tenderest beef tenderloin you'll get in a Japanese restaurant); **Nimono**, cooked okra and clams; and a fiery hot **Conch Shell**, which is a clam spiced with the hot stuff. The food is extremely fresh, and the chef does not overdo the *shoyu* (soy sauce) nor overly complicate his entrées with a lot of extras. For dessert, you get dried fruit with a citrus overlay.

While changing periodically, the menus at **Makoto** are carefully chosen and the food is always expertly prepared. Because it's so small and so good, it's a good idea to call ahead in advance for reservations.

MATUBA

Two Locations: 4918 Cordell Ave., Bethesda, MD (301/652-7449). **Nearest Metro:** Bethesda on the Red Line; 2915 Columbia Pike, Arlington, VA (703/521-2811). **Nearest Metro:** Pentagon on the BLue Line. **Hours for both:** M-F, 11:30 am - 2:00 pm, 5:30 pm - 10:00 pm; Sat.-Sun., 5:30 pm - 10:00 pm. **Credit Cards:** AE, MC, V. **Price:** INEXPENSIVE.

Matuba is not fancy, but does offer consistently good food, particularly sushi and donburi, the latter dish not readily available in many area Japanese restaurants. And they do it for half the price of other, bigger-name places.

The sushi and sashimi appetizers are fresh, and Matuba features a full range of choices. They also offer both a hot **Fried Bean Curd** and a **Cold Bean Curd**, both simply prepared and delicious.

The entrées, each served with your choice of either **Miso** (clear soybean) **Soup** or **Matuba** (chicken) **Soup** and rice, include larger assortments of fresh sushi and sashimi, but other winners are **Salmon Teriyaki** and **Tonkatsu**, a breaded, deep-fried pork cutlet served with a soy-based sauce. You can also do the sushi a la carte; two of my favorites that are hard to get elsewhere are the **Spicy Tuna Roll** and the **Bagel Roll** (Cream Cheese and Smoked Salmon sushi - further evidence that the Japanese may well be the lost tribe of Israel).

The **Donburi** dishes are very well done here. Two of the better entrées are the **Katsu Donburi**, deep-fried pork cutlet and egg cooked in soy sauce, topped with onions and scallions; and the **Oyako Donburi**, the same idea as the Katsu Donburi, but sliced boneless chicken is substituted for the pork.

The secret to any good sushi place, it should go without saying, is getting fresh fish and not killing it with too much experimentation. The nice thing about *Matuba* is that they know how to prepare good sushi without charging an arm and a leg. Ten Thousand Victories!

SAKURA PALACE

7926 Georgia Ave., Silver Spring, MD (301/587-7070). **Nearest Metro:** Silver Spring on the Red Line. **Hours:** T-F, 11:30 am - 2:30 pm, 5:30 pm - 10:00 pm;Sat.-Sun., 5:00 pm - 10:00 pm. **Credit Cards:** MC, V. **Price:** MODERATE.

This pleasant if somewhat dark restaurant is one of the favorites of many local Japanese. Perhaps it's because you can count on fresh sushi at reasonable prices, or maybe it's the homey (though frequently slow) service. Or maybe it's the free salad bar with dinner, unusual in a Japanese place. Whatever the reason, **Sakura Palace** is one of the better Japanese restaurants in suburban Maryland.

The salad comes with a tangy dressing called **gomasu**, a little strange but actually pretty tasty; the **Miso Soup** is all right but rather plain. The **Sushi** appetizers are great; fresh and served in generous portions. More and more Japanese restaurants are now serving some different kinds of sushi, like the **Spicy Tuna Roll**, which packs quite a wallop, in addition to the old standbys like regular tuna (**Maguro**), **Cucumber Rolls**, and perhaps the best version of **Daikon** (pickled radish) around these parts.

For entrées, some of my favorites include the **Salmon Teriyaki**, a broiled salmon dish with teriyaki sauce; **Yosenabe**, an assortment of seafood and vegetables in a hot pot; **Tonkatsu**, a deep-fried breaded pork filet; and the **Negimaki**, chicken or beef wrapped in onions and scallions and seasoned with *shoyu* (Japenese soy sauce).

If you're up for a larger dish, I'd highly recommend the **Shabu-Shabu** (the word doesn't mean anything per se; it's a description of the beef swishing in the soup). It's a large broth with lean steak slices, cooked together with cabbage, onions, scallions, bamboo shoots, and mushrooms. It's one of the house specialties, and justly so.

Considering how expensive most Japanese restaurants are, **Sakura Palace** comes in with very good quality, a nice presentation, and a reasonable price.

TACHIBANA

4050 Lee Highway, Arlington, VA (703/528-1122). **Nearest Metro:** N/A.
Hours: M-Th, 11:30 am - 2:00 pm, 5:00 pm - 10:00 pm; F, 11:30 am - 2:00
pm, 5:00 pm - 10:30 pm; Sat., 5:00 pm - 10:30 pm; closed Sun. **Credit Cards:**
AE, DC, MC, Most, V. **Price:** MODERATE.

Tachibana is a great choice, whether you live in the Virginia 'burbs or are
just looking for good value, a nice selection, and consistently superior food.
While the dining room is relatively large, I would suggest you make reservations on weekend nights.

If you like sushi or sashimi, this is the place for you. Even if you're in the
mood for something more substantive (i.e., something cooked!) for the main
event, try one of the **Sushi** appetizers. You won't be sorry. It's always fresh
and out of this world! The **Age-Dofu** (pronounced a-gay do-fu) is also very
good; it's deep fried tofu in a soupy broth with grated ginger and radish.

The **Tempura** (deep fried vegetable and seafood batter dishes) and
Katsu (breaded and deep fried pork, chicken, or fish cutlets) are both excellent
here: not too greasy or heavy. My favorite "pot dish," a sizable meal cooked
in an earthenware pot, is **Shabu-Shabu**, but you have to order it 24 hours in
advance. Shabu-Shabu is a mixture of vegetables and thinly sliced beef, served
with a tasty dipping sauce. There's something about the preparation in the
pot that gives these dishes a special, delicious flavor. You can't go wrong with
the **Nigimaki** (sometimes spelled negamaki at other Japanese restaurants),
which is rolled beef or chicken with scallion, grilled in a teriyaki sauce.

The noodle dishes are also very good here. Try either of the **Udon** dishes
(noodles in soup with cooked seafood or vegetables); if you want to eat an
authentically-prepared Japanese dish that is a favorite of many Japanese
diners, order the **Ochazuke**, a bowl of rice topped with either seaweed,
salmon, cod roe or preserved plum. Don't drink the green tea accompanying
the dish; pour it over the top and go to town.

Overall, *Tachibana's* service, value, and prices make it one of our better
Japanese eateries.

TAKO GRILL

7756 Wisconsin Ave., Bethesda, MD (301/652-7030). **Nearest Metro:** Bethesda, on the Red Line. **Hours:** Lunch, M-F, 11:30 am - 2:00 pm; Dinner, M-Th, 5:30 pm - 9:45 pm, F-Sat., 5:30 am - 10:15 pm; closed Sun. **Credit Cards:** AE, MC, V. **Price:** MODERATE.

This is a hip Japanese restaurant. Waiters and waitresses are mostly American, not Japanese, and there is a much younger feel to the place than at most other area restaurants. There are no reservations, however, and waiting 20-30 minutes is not unusual on a weekend night. But the food at **Tako Grill** is worth the wait.

The **Sushi** and especially the **Sashimi** dishes are quite good; they meet the freshness and preparation test easily. The **Miso Soup** and **Bean Sprout Salad** are a little more tasty than the usual soup and salad combo at Japanese restaurants. But for something a bit different, try the **Roba-tayaki**, a Japanese-style grill featuring vegetables, shiitake mushrooms, and whole crispy fish. The fried **Tempura** dishes don't suffer from excess grease, and the simple **Teriyaki** dishes, with chicken or beef, are good choices too.

My top pick, though, apart from the excellent sashimi here, is the **Negamaki**, beef rolled in scallions. It's tender and juicy, with just the right amount of *shoyu* and seasonings. A little green tea with your meal or after dinner nicely complements your meal.

Tako Grill is a fun place that does the basics well. If you don't mind an occasional wait, you'll be rewarded with a great Japanese dinner for a most reasonable price.

STRAITS OF MALAYA

1836 18th St., Washington, DC (202/483-1483). **Nearest Metro:** Dupont Circle on the Red Line. **Hours:** Lunch, Noon - 2:00 pm daily; Dinner, Sun.-Th, 5:30 pm - 10:30 pm, F-Sat., 5:30 pm - 11:00 pm. **Credit Cards:** AE, CB, DC, MC, V. **Price:** MODERATE.

Straits of Malaya serves top-notch Southeast Asian cuisine in an attractive setting. Malaysian delicacies are not well known in America, but I'll wager you'll want to learn more about this fanstastic cuisine after eating here. It's a pity that there aren't any other Malaysian places around town.

You've got one soup and nine appetizers to choose from, all of which are well worth trying. Start with the **Laksa**, one of the most delicious soups I've ever had. It's a hot and spicy noodle soup, made with rice stick noodles, shrimp, chicken, bean sprouts, egg, coconut milk and coriander. The **Rojak** is great too, a cold salad made with cucumbers, pineapple, carrots, and jicama, all marinated in a somewhat spicy sauce made from shrimp paste and ground peanuts. You might also want to consider the **Chicken Satay and Rice Cakes**, since Malaysians (and Indonesians) do satays better than anyone else; the accompanying peanut sauce is fantastic and on the spicy side. And if you're a fan of fried bean curd, try the **Tofu with Chili and Peanut Sauce**, which is light and un-greasy but packs a nice wallop in the spice department.

There are so many good entrées here that it's hard to steer you to just a few, but here goes. **Cha Kway Teow** is tops on my list; broad, flat rice noodles stir-fried with chicken, chili paste, mushroom sauce, bean sprouts, onions, and snow peas. You can taste the Chinese influences but you know it's not quite Chinese. The **Chicken with Basil** is a simple dish, but they sure do it right here. The **Poh Pia** is a fun choice, with the vegetable jicama shredded and stir-fried with bean sprouts, chicken, dried shrimp, and leeks. Like the Chinese *Moo Shu Pork*, it comes with thin pancakes and a plum sauce. The **Bawang Sambal Udang** is a great shrimp and onion dish, cooked in a spicy sauce featuring chili and tamarind, and the **Nasi Goreng** is a mildly spiced chicken breast served over Malaysian fried rice, green peas, bean sprouts, and onions.

It's rare that I've gone to a place, no matter how good, and loved every dish on the menu. *Straits of Malaya* is one of those places!

CAFÉ ASIA

1134 19th St., NW, Washington, DC (202/659-2696). **Nearest Metro:** Dupont Circle on the Red Line. **Hours:** M-F, 11:30am -10:00 pm; Sat, Noon- 10:00 pm; closed Sun. **Credit Cards:** AE, MC, V. **Price:** MODERATE.

Café Asia is a fun, stylish restaurant with friendly service and good down-home pan-Asian cookin'. If you want to impress a client or a date with decor and presentation, you'll probably want to go to Germaine's. But you'll pay for that upscale approach dearly; at **Café Asia**, you'll get a great meal for a lot less moolah. The featured cuisines are Indonesian, Thai, Vietnamese, Chinese, Singaporean and Japanese. For my money, the Indonesian, Vietnamese, and Thai dishes are the best here.

For appetizers and soup, start with the **Vietnamese Shrimp on Sugar Cane** or the **Spicy Chinese Ravioli**, which are pork dumplings with a spicy sauce made from ground red peppers. The **Thai soups** are the best here; try the **Shrimp Coconut Milk Soup** for a non-spicy dish, or the **Spicy Chicken Lemon Grass Soup** if you do like it hot. The salads are good but not great.

For chicken entrées, my recommendations are the **Thai Chicken with Basil Leaves** or the **Indonesian Grilled Chicken** (prepared with sweet soy sauce from Indonesia and galanga, a wild ginger root). For beef and pork, go for the **Spicy Beef in Coconut Sauce** (diced beef cooked in brown curry paste and coconut milk, served with vegetables); the **Tongkatsu**, a Japanese dish of fried breaded pork cutlet, served with Japanese plum sauce and vegetables; or the **Vietnamese Lemon Grass Beef** (pan-fried ribeye steak cooked in lemon grass and French butter). For seafood, try the **Indonesian Grilled Shrimp** (made the same way as the Indonesian Grilled Chicken) or the **Thai Spicy Shrimp Curry** (shrimp and vegetables cooked in coconut milk and spicy red curry paste).

And if you just want some veggies, try the **Chinese Style Tofu with Garlic Sauce** (their version of *Ma-Po Tofu*) or **Thai Spicy Vegetables Curry** (vegetables cooked in coconut milk and Thai curry paste). If you want a good sampling of different Asian cuisines, this is one of the best places in DC to visit.

GERMAINE'S

2400 Wisconsin Ave., NW, Washington, DC (202/965-1185). **Nearest Metro:** N/A. **Hours:** M-Th, 11:30 am - 2:30 pm, 5:30 pm - 10:00 pm; F, 11:30 am - 2:30 pm, 5:30 pm - 11:00 pm; Sat., 5:30 pm - 11:00 pm; Sun., 5:30 pm - 10:00 pm. **Credit Cards:** AE, CB, MC, Trans-Media, V. **Price:** EXPENSIVE.

Germaine's was, for years on end, the best gourmet Asian restaurant in the area, and the owner is widely credited with starting the pan-Asian trend in the US. But serious competition has emerged of late for the gourmet Asian restaurant dollar. The bill of fare still titillates, but, the high quality notwithstanding, the price tag has gotten pretty steep.

The decor is classy, with the photographs on the walls adding to the pan-Asian atmosphere. Before you delve into the goodies, a word on the barkeep: he knows his stuff. Whether you're ordering a Sapphire Bombay Gibson straight-up, extra dry, or any other mixed drink, Germaine's will not disappoint. For starters, try the **Cold Szechuan Noodles**, a spicy noodle appetizer with a delicious hot sauce; the **Korean Shredded Beef** (*Gogi Bokun*), also hot; and any of the satés served with their homemade spicy peanut sauce. The soups are not out of the ordinary, with the exception of **Pho Ga**, a worthy Vietnamese chicken and rice noodle soup cooked with Chinese parsley, scallions, hot peppers and *nuoc mam* (fish sauce).

On the entrée front, I have always liked their version of **Basil Beef**, a spicy Thai sautéed shredded beef dish with basil leaves and hot red peppers. Other picks include the **Pork in Ginger Sauce**; the **Firecracker Shrimp**, stir-fried shrimp with diced bamboo and onions, cooked hot and spicy; or the milder **Shrimp Saigon Sauce**, stir-fried in a garlic and ginger sauce. Honorable mentions also go to the Japanese **Sesame Chicken**, lightly battered, deep-fried chicken cooked with sesame sauce, and the **Singapore-Style Noodles**, seasoned and spiced sliced beef cooked with vegetables and rice noodles.

For dessert, there's usually fresh fruit, but if you haven't tried **Lychee Nut Ice Cream**, now's the time. It's a perfect way to end a sumptuous repast at what is still one of the best - if priciest - Asian restaurants in town.

PAN-ASIAN NOODLES AND GRILL

Two locations: 1018 Vermont Ave., NW, Washington, DC (202/783-8899). **Nearest Metro:** McPherson Square on the Blue Line. **Hours:** M-F, 11:30 am - 9:00 pm; closed Sat.-Sun.; and 2020 P St., NW, Washington, DC (202/872-8889). **Nearest Metro:** Dupont Circle on the Red Line. **Hours:** M-Sat., 11:30 am - 2:30 pm, 5:30 - 10:00 pm; F-Sat. dinner until 11:00 pm; Sun., 5:30 pm - 11:00 pm. **Credit Cards:** AE, CB, DC, MC, V. **Price:** INEXPENSIVE.

Noodles from around Asia is the theme here, and most of the time **Pan-Asian Noodles and Grill** delivers. The location on P Street is more of a neighborhood hangout and on the cramped side, while the roomier Vermont Ave. place does far more of a lunch and after-work crowd.

But cramped or not, **Pan-Asian** sure knows what they're doing. A good way to pick out an interesting meal is to order several of the various cuisines represented. Start with the **Singapore Nuggets**, crab meat and minced chicken wrapped in deep-fried bean curd peels; the **Asian Ravioli**, steamed dumplings filled with either meat or vegetables and a hot Taiwanese beef sauce; and the **Southeast Asian Spring Rolls** (crispy rolls stuffed with ground chicken, mushrooms, and bean thread noodles), which is a variation on the Vietnamese **Cha Gio** - which is also good here.

A delicious entrée is the **Filipino Grilled Chicken**, a grilled half chicken marinated in lime juice, black pepper, dark soy sauce, and garlic, served in their own tangy "Java Sauce." The best noodle dishes (and I should stress that I've yet to be disappointed by any of their noodle entrées) are the **Drunken Noodles**, steamed flat noodles topped with stir-fried minced chicken in a hot basil sauce; **Cozy Noodles**, a cold noodle dish with shredded chicken and veggies, tossed in a mildly spicy peanut curry sauce; and the **Chapchae Noodles**, straight from Korea, a dish of stir-fried green bean noodles with beef, scallions, and assorted sliced vegetables.

After slurping down all those noodles, chances are you'll be in the mood for some dessert. Anyone who's had the coconut rice and mango dessert (and plenty of people have, judging by the number of folks who recommended it to me!) will agree that this is not your usual, too-sweet rice pudding knock-off.

The bottom line: if you want a great noodle meal, **Pan-Asian** is the place to go.

BUSARA

2340 Wisconsin Avenue, NW, Washington (202/337-2340). *Nearest Metro:* N/A. *Hours:* Lunch, M-F, 11:30 am - 3:00 pm, Sat.-Sun., 11:30 am - 4:00 pm; Dinner, Sun-Th, 5:00 pm - 11:00 pm; F-Sat., 5:00 pm - Midnight. *Credit Cards:* AE, MC, V. *Price:* MODERATE.

Busara, which means "Blue Topaz" in Thai, bills itself as "Siamese Cuisine." *Busara* has a very modern, neon look; I half expected to see black-light posters of the King and Queen hanging from the walls when I first walked in. But its cool Western trappings aside, Busara is well worth the visit. While somewhat more expensive than its neighbor and sister restaurant Ploy a block away, *Busara* is well worth exploring.

Busara has an extensive menu. For starters, if you're in the mood for soup, try either the spicy **Tom Ka Gai** (chicken pieces in coconut soup) or the equally hot **Tom Yum Goong**, a hot and sour lemon grass soup with shrimp. The Thai salads here are very good, as are most appetizers, particularly the **Larb Gai** (spicy minced chicken in lime juice) and the **Satay** — but the **Crispy Spring Rolls** are inconsistent and greasy as often as not.

The noodle dishes here are very good, particularly the **Pad Thai**, stir-fried noodles with shrimp, tofu, crushed peanuts, bean sprouts, scallions and egg, and the **Pad Woon Sen**, cellophane noodles stir-fried with shrimp, pork, mushrooms, and assorted vegetables. There are also seven vegetarian entrées; my favorite is the **Spicy Garden** (veggies sautéed in a hot and spicy bean sauce). The fish and seafood dishes are excellent here; if you're hungry or in a group, order the **Crispy Whole Flounder**, which you can make as hot or mild as you like. Another favorite is the **Naked Shrimp**, a moderately spicy serving of grilled black tiger shrimp. The chicken and pork dishes here are generally good, with one notable exception: the **Gang Gai**, chicken in a too-soupy green curry sauce and basil, is just not up to par. My favorite "Special Entree" is the **Moo Yang**, marinated pork grilled in a nicely spiced tamarind sauce served with brown rice and skewered grilled vegetables.

The service at *Busara* is friendly and efficient, and the barkeep knows how to make a drink. All in all, one of the better Thai restaurants in the area.

CAJUN BANGKOK

907 King St., Alexandria, VA (703/836-0038). **Nearest Metro:** King St. on the Blue Line. **Hours:** M-Th, 5:00 - 10:00 pm; F-Sat., 11:00 am - 11:00 pm; Sun., Noon - 10:00 pm. **Credit Cards:** AE, MC, V. **Price:** MODERATE.

What a great idea to merge these two sensational cuisines so noted for their hot and spicy possibilities! **Cajun Bangkok** does an admirable job in both areas; Louisianans and Thais need not fear this particular experiment. Perhaps **Cajun Bangkok** will inspire other adventurous ethnic cuisine pairings.

I'm more partial to the Thai dishes here, so I'm including it in the Thai section, but some of the Cajun choices are top-notch as well.

Start with the **Magic Wings**, a spicy Cajun dish of fried chicken wings, a little greasy at times but delicious nonetheless; the fantastic **Crying Tiger**, grilled sirloin steak with a hot crushed red pepper sauce; and the **Meang Kham**, a mostly Thai combination of roasted coconut and roasted peanuts, limes, ginger, red onions, dried shrimps, red peppers, collard greens and ginger sauce. This is a rare treat; the mix of flavors is superb, and, best of all, you get to play with your food as you make the collard greens into a sandwich of sorts.

For Cajun entrées, try the **Cajun Bangkok Gumbo**, sautéed shrimp, chicken, and sausage cooked in a hot gumbo sauce; and the **Pepper Shrimp and Chicken Picata**, a sautéed shrimp and chicken dish cooked in a hot sauce of black pepper and lemon butter.

On the Thai side of the menu, my picks are the **Red Curry Beef Panang**, beef chunks cooked in red curry sauce mixed with coconut milk; the **Shrimp Pad Thai**, a spicy version of this Thai classic, prepared here with stir-fried rice noodles, shrimp, scallions, bean sprouts, and topped with crushed peanuts; and the **Mooh-Aroy**, a chili pork loin barbecued in a hot chili sauce.

Are there better places to get Thai and Cajun? Of course. But nowhere else around here can you get the two together, and sample both cuisines at the same time. I only hope they add some more creative dishes to what is presently a somewhat small menu.

CRYSTAL THAI

4819 Arlington Blvd., Arlington, VA (703/522-1311). *Nearest Metro:* N/A.
Hours: M-Th, 11:30 am - 10:30 pm; F-Sat., 11:30 am - 11:00 pm; Sun., Noon
- 10:00 pm. *Credit Cards:* AE, CB, DC, DV, MC, V. *Price:* MODERATE.

Located in the Arlington Forest Shopping Center on Rt. 50, *Crystal Thai*
has become part of my "troika" of the area's three great Thai restaurants, the
other two being Duangrat's and Bangkok Vientiane, with Rabieng, Busara,
and several others trailing closely behind ... what a great race! Crystal Thai
scores big on all counts: quality, value, service, and decor.

To begin with, try the **Yum Kuen Khoew**, a mouth-watering special
appetizer not always on the menu (but ask them to make it anyway) consisting
of shrimp, chili peppers, lemon grass, lime juice, kaffir lime leaves and mint
leaves. The **Larb Gai** is also excellent, made as hot or mild as you like it, as
is the **Yum Pla Dook Foo**, which is a cold crispy catfish served in a hot brown
sauce. And the **Kai Yang Thai Style** should not be missed either: marinated
white chicken breastgrilled over a slow fire, served with sticky rice and a hot
dipping sauce.

The soups are as good as any in the area, especially the **Tom Yum
Goong**, shrimp and mushrooms in a hot and sour soup with lemon grass and
Thai spices.

I've ordered most of the entrées on this menu, and I haven't gone wrong
yet. Limiting my top picks to just a few, however, I'd go with the **Kai Pad Pick
Krapao**, a spicy stir-fried chicken, sautéed with basil leaf and red chili peppers;
the **Green Curry Chicken**, chicken chunks with green curry, bamboo shoots,
and basil leaves, cooked in a grease-free coconut milk; and the **Panang Beef**,
beef chunks cooked in red curry sauce, coconut milk, and fresh basil.

The noodle dishes are routinely spectacular, if I can use those two words
in combination! The best of the best are **Pad Talay**, a semi-hot sautéed rice
noodle dish mixed with seafood, hot chili sauce, and basil; and the **Pad Thai**,
made here with tofu (bean curd) instead of bean sprouts.

I can't say enough good things about this place, and I don't want to be
accused of raving (any more than I already am accused of it), so I'll close by
urging you intrepid eaters out there to try *Crystal Thai*.

DUANGRAT'S

6878 Leesburg Pike, Falls Church, VA (703/820-5775). **Nearest Metro:** N/A. **Hours:** M-Th, 11:30 am - 2:30 pm, 5:00 pm - 10:30 pm; F, 11:30 am - 2:30 pm, 5:00 pm - 11;00 pm; Sat., 11:30 am - 11:00 pm; Sun., 11:30 am - 11:00 pm. **Credit Cards:** AE, CB, DC, MC, V. **Price:** MODERATE.

Duangrat's, two of whose lovely waitresses are featured on the front cover of this guide, is one of the two best Thai restaurants in this city. The service is always efficient and courteous.

There is a big selection of appetizers here, both cold and hot; try the **Larb** (cold spicy chicken or beef sautéed in lemon juice, ginger, and peanuts) or the **Mee Grob** (sometimes spelled elsewhere as Mee Krob), which is fried vermicelli with cold minced pork cooked in a sweet and sour sauce. For hot appetizers, the **Spring Rolls** are very good, as is the **Gold Sachet Duangrat** (shrimp and pork cooked with sweet corn and Thai spices, deep fried and served wrapped together in tofu skin). The soups are always good here; the **Tom Yum** is a typical Thai soup, with shrimp or chicken in a broth of lemon grass, chili, and lemon juice. The **Chicken Galanka** is also a classic, featuring coconut milk and galanka (more commonly galanga) root, similar to ginger.

The specials change routinely here, but usually **Bhram** is on the list, and I highly recommend it (you can get it all the time at **Duangrat's** excellent sister restaurant around the corner, Rabieng). It is considered an "Old Thai" dish, and it's hard to get around these parts; it's a hot chicken dish sautéed in garlic and cooked in a spicy peanut sauce, served on Napa cabbage and topped with crispy shallots. The **Beef Basil** is a clear winner, as is the **Pork with Fried Garlic** and the **Pork (or Beef) With Ginger Shreds**.

If you like curry, try the **Panang Chicken**, which is prepared in a panang curry paste and coconut milk. The seafood dishes are particularly good here; I'd recommend the **Hot Dish Talay Thai** if you want something spicy. It's a combination dish with various seafood, mushrooms, bamboo shoots and stir-fried in fresh basil and a great hot sauce. All the shrimp and fish dishes are very good; if you're feeling adventurous, the **Stuffed Squid Siam Bay** (squid stuffed with shrimp and pork and fried in garlic and white pepper) is delicious. There are six vegetarian dishes on the menu, and one of the best **Phad Thai** offerings anywhere (this is the standard stir-fried noodle dish with shrimp, egg, and bean sprouts).

Duangrat's has classical Thai dancing on weekend nights, so reservations make sense, even though there are two floors and plenty of room. If you're looking for a genuine class act, this is the place.

DUSIT

2404 University Blvd., Wheaton, MD (301/949-4140). **Nearest Metro:** Wheaton on the Red Line. **Hours:** Sun.-Th, 11:30 am - 10:00 pm; F-Sat., 11:30 am - 11:00 pm; closed Mon. **Credit Cards:** AE, MC, V. **Price:** INEXPENSIVE.

For those of you living out in the Maryland 'burbs who don't want to make the trek out to Northern Virginia or into DC for some great Thai food, fear not: you've got an excellent Thai restaurant in Wheaton called **Dusit**. In addition to a modern pink-and-neon interior and friendly service, **Dusit** boasts great value and fine food.

Appetizers and soups are plentiful here. The **Hot and Sour Beef or Chicken (Larb)** is a delicious hot ground beef or chicken made with mint, lemon, onion, and lettuce; it's a hot dish worthy of the two star designation the owners call "very spicy hot." The **Hot Bean Thread Salad (Yum Wun Sen)** is one of the reasons I love Thai food: semi-spicy shrimp, chicken, and thin vermicelli, flavored with lemon, chili sauce, and onions. You've got 18 other worthy choices to start off your meal, plus some very good Thai soups, in particular the **Gulf of Siam**, a clear hot and sour soup made with straw mushrooms, seafood, lemon grass, and chilis.

Their curry dishes are good but not out of the ordinary, with the exception of the **Country Curry (Kaeng Pa)**, a hot curry dish made with your choice of chicken, beef, or pork which is well above standard fare. The **Pad Thai** and other noodle dishes are good, but not the reason to come here; the reason you want to come here are the chicken, pork, and seafood dishes, entrées like the succulent **Chicken with String Bean and Curry Sauce**, a hopping **Pork with Sweet Basil** (stir-fried in chili and garlic), the **Dusit Shrimp** (stir-fried shrimp in garlic sauce and white pepper), or the **Squid with Hot Chili Pepper** (stir-fried with scallions and mushrooms). These picks can hold their own against similar dishes at the very best Thai restaurants in the area.

Dusit is yet another feather in the cap of our area's great Thai restaurants.

<u>PLOY</u>

2218 Wisconsin Ave., NW, Washington, DC (202/337-2324). **Nearest Metro:** N/A. **Hours:** M-Th, 11:30 am - 3:00 pm, 5:00 pm - 10:30 pm; F, 11:30 am - 3:00 pm, 5:00 pm - 11:00 pm; Sat., Noon - 11:00 pm; Sun., Noon - 3:30 pm, 5:00 pm - 10:30 pm. **Credit Cards:** AE, DC, MC, V. **Price:** MODERATE.

Since **Ploy** opened some years ago, a number of first-rate Thai restaurants have opened, keeping the chefs here on their toes. **Ploy** may not be the best Thai place in the area, but it remains a solid fixture on the scene, offering good food at good value. Decor is modern and sleek.

Start with **Mee-Krob**, a better treatment of this crispy noodle appetizer with pork, shrimp, and a sweet dipping sauce, than at many other Thai joints. Other top appetizers include the **Yum Talay**, a hot and spicy salad of shrimp, scallops, squid, and vegetables, and the **Moo Yang**, pork marinated in white pepper and garlic in a hot sauce. And for soup, you won't find the **Kang Som Goong** at too many other restaurants; it's a shrimp and vegetable soup cooked with tamarind and curry sauce.

There are a number of excellent vegetarian dishes here, mostly featuring tofu and various sauces (peanut, garlic, sweet and sour). Other recommendations are the **Ploy Glass Noodles**, transparent (glass) noodles mixed with pork, shrimp, egg, and black mushrooms; the **Goong-Oob**, which, besides having a great name, is a delicious cellophane noodle dish with shrimp and vegetables in a hot chili sauce; and **Katiem Pik Thai**, your choice of pork or chicken sautéed with white pepper, garlic, and broccoli.

For me, it's a happy coincidence that most of my favorite Thai restaurants have different strengths. **Ploy** has its share of superb dishes and its share of so-so dishes, but on balance you'll get reliably good Thai cooking.

RABIENG

5892 Leesburg Pike, Falls Church, VA (703/671-4222). **Nearest Metro:** N/A (Rabieng is right around the corner from Duangrats, its sister restaurant). **Hours:** 11:30 am - 10:00 pm, daily. **Credit Cards:** AE, DC, MC, V.**Price:** MODERATE.

Rabieng is so good it gives Duangrat's a serious run for its money. *Rabieng's* hook is that it's "Country Thai," which to you and me translates to northern Thai. The dining area is very small, with a soft ambiance perfect for romantic dining.

While the menu offers Thai classics familiar to any who have ventured into Thai restaurants before, go to Rabieng to sample the northern specialties that are non-existent in most Thai restaurants. Start with **Tidbit**, a pork dish in coconut sauce served over fried, crispy sticky rice and topped with crushed nuts; or, if you're in the market for something hot, try the **Fried Cashew Nuts**, pan-fried cashew nuts with butter, chili and spring onion. The **Esan Sausage** is great, either as an appetizer or a main dish; it's a grilled sausage made with a blend of pork, rice, and lemon grass.

Again, either as a first course or an entrée, the **Spicy Noodle Soup with Beef and Bean Sprouts** is always a good bet. The **Bhram**, also available at Duangrat's, is worth the price of gas for those of us who don;t live nearby; it's a hot chicken dish sautéed in garlic and cooked in a spicy peanut sauce, served on Napa cabbage and topped with crispy shallots.

In the audacious and doughty category, a somewhat gamey (but nevertheless very tasty) dish is the **Panang Boar**, which is sautéed boar (wild piggies) cooked in curry paste and coconut milk and served on a bed of rice. The **Chicken Green Curry** is on the hot side, prepared in a green curry sauce and basil; it's served over rice and noodles. You can also get virtually any dish you can get at Duangrat's, with the same high quality and good service.

Rabieng is a great addition to the Thai food scene in the metropolitan area. I only hope they add a few more "country" dishes for our culinary pleasure.

RINCOME THAI

3030 Columbia Pike, Arlington, VA (703/979-0144 or -0145). *Nearest Metro:* N/A. *Hours:* M-F, 11:00 am - 11:00 pm; Sat.-Sun., Noon - 11:00 pm. *Credit Cards:* AE, DC, MC, V. *Price:* INEXPENSIVE.

Not much on decor, *Rincome Thai* does several things well, but most especially making their food as hot as you can stand it. If you're looking for a good - sometimes outstanding - spicy hot meal, this is the ticket. But they can also cool it down for you too, so you get the full Thai flavoring without all that heat. The appetizer, soup, and entrée selections are extensive.

You might want to start with the **Yum Voon-Sen**, the best version of this I've encountered; it's a plate of silver noodles with minced pork, shrimp, hot peppers, onions, and lime juice. The **Larb** (minced chicken or beef with hot peppers, onions, and lime juice) is good but not great, as is the **Som-Tum**, a papaya salad with tomatoes, hot peppers, dried shrimp, green beans, and lime juice. I find the soups a little more average, but my favorite here is the **Tom-Kha Kai**, chicken soup with coconut milk, chiles, lemon grass, mushrooms, galanga root and lime juice.

For entrées, their **basil leaves and peppers** dishes are excellent; they come with chicken, beef, squid, or pork. I'd also strongly recommend the **Pla Lad Prig**, a spicy, crispy whole fish topped with red chili peppers, mushrooms, and garlic sauce. Other superb dishes here are the **Pa-Nang**, a hot red curry sauce made with coconut milk poured over either chicken, beef, or pork; a good **Pad Thai**; and the **Seafood Combination**, a mixture of sautéed shrimp, scallops, squid, crab claws, and mussels, topped with fresh mint leaves and hot peppers.

Coffee and desserts are nothing to write home about, but for those more interested in the main event, *Rincome Thai* has plenty to offer.

SALA THAI

2016 P Street, NW, Washington (202/872-1144). **Nearest Metro:** Dupont Circle on the Red Line. **Hours:** Sun.-Th, 5:00 pm - 10:30 pm; F-Sat., 5:00 pm - 11:00 pm. **Credit Cards:** AE, DC, MC, V. **Price:** MODERATE.

Sala Thai is yet another of the many good restaurants along P Street. I'm not sure I'd say there are any terrific standouts here, other than the standard **Pad Thai**, but the watchword here is consistency. Some of the better Thai restaurants seem to run hot and cold - and even the best of places will let you down occasionally - but *Sala Thai* ususally runs true to form.

Among the better appetizers are the **Tod Mun**, a fried curry fish cake served with a semi-spicy dipping sauce featuring *nam pla* (fish sauce) and scallions. But don't let the name mislead you; it's the least fishy version of this specialty around. The **Yum Talay**, however - a salad of shrimp, squid, and scallops spiced with hot chilis and lemon juice - could stand more heat and more pizzaz. I like the **Nam Sod** better (minced pork with ginger in a hot sauce of spices and lemon juice), or one of the soups, especially the **Tom Ka Gai**, chicken in coconut milk and galanga root.

For entrées, in addition to the aforementioned **Pad Thai**, try the **Kee Mao**, flat rice noodles cooked with minced beef, chicken, or seafood, in a spicy basil sauce. If you want it hot, you'll have to ask them to pour it on, otherwise you'll get a relatively bland version of what can be an outstanding dish. Other good noodles dishes here are the **Pad Woon Sen** and **Mee Ka Thi**, the former being cellophane noodles wokked up with shrimp, pork, egg, and black mushrooms, the latter being thin noodles and shrimp, pork, and tofu, cooked in coconut milk.

The seafood dishes should not be overlooked either. Try the **Sea Madness**, a combo of shrimp, squid, and scallops cooked with vegetables and basil in a moderately hot red sauce. Or go with my top pick here, the excellent **Crispy Whole Flounder**, grilled in a chili and garlic sauce. You won't worry about bones here, and the flounder practically melts off your fork.

So many new and great Thai restaurants have opened since 1987 (when *Sala Thai* flung open its doors) that it no longer has the caché it once did. But I'm happy to return here periodically and get a good, and sometimes great, Thai noodle or seafood dish.

STAR OF SIAM

Three locations: 1136 19th St., NW, Washington, DC (202/785-2838). **Nearest Metro:** Farragut North on the Red Line; 2446 18th St., NW, Washington, DC (202/986-4133). **Nearest Metro:** Dupont Circle on the Red Line; and 1735 N. Lynn St., Rosslyn (703/524-1208). **Nearest Metro:** Rosslyn on the Blue/Orange Line. **Hours for all three:** M-Sat., 11:30 am - 11:00 pm; Sun., 4:00 pm - 10:00 pm. **Credit Cards:** AE, CB, DC, MC, V. **Price:** MODERATE.

The three **Star of Siam** restaurants serve very good, reliable Thai food. The dining rooms are bright and airy, particularly the one in Adams Morgan (the 18th St. location) that features a small Thai-style dining area where you sit on brightly-colored cushions. The service is friendly and efficient; the menu is large, featuring a good variety of Thai classics.

The **Larb Gai** appetizer (semi-spicy minced chicken with lime juice, chili sauce, and Thai spices) is primo here. I'd also recommend the even hotter **Yam Neau**, which is done better here than most other places; it's grilled sliced beef with onions, cucumbers, lime juice and hot chili. The soups are also good (if not spectacular) for starters, particularly the **Tom Yam Gai**, a spicy chicken soup cooked in lemon grass, with lime juice and hot chiles.

For entrées, the curry dishes really shine here. Two of my picks in this area are the **Panang Goong**, shrimp cooked in a red curry sauce, coconut milk, and basil leaves, and the **Gang Keo-Wan**, one of the better green curry dishes in town, prepared with chicken or beef and coconut milk, bamboo shoots, and eggplant. For a mild alternative to these hot dishes, try the **Gai Pad King**, a simple but tasty chicken with fresh ginger and onions, or the **Pad Thai**, made here with rice noodles and chicken, shrimp, bean sprouts, and egg, and topped with crushed peanuts. As at other Thai places, most of the dishes that are marked hot and spicy can be considerably toned down upon request.

Star of Siam is one of the better choices among the growing number of Thai restaurants in the Washington area. If you're looking for an especially good curry dish, this should be one of your top choices.

CAFÉ DALAT

3143 Wilson Blvd., Arlington, VA (703/276-0935). *Nearest Metro:* Clarendon on the Blue/Orange Line. *Hours:* Sun.-Th, 11:00 am - 9:30 pm; F-Sat., 11:00 am - 10:30 pm. *Credit Cards:* MC, V. *Price:* INEXPENSIVE-TO-MODERATE.

While not big on ambiance, *Café Dalat* is big on good food, well seasoned and, if you ask for it, hot and spicy. The service is quick and friendly, and the prices are very reasonable.

If you like your vittles hot and piquant, start with the **Ga xao lan**, their sautéed five-spice chicken. Covered with a delicious creamy yellow sauce, this appetizer packs quite a wallop. If you prefer a milder beginning to your meal, go with either the **Goi Cuon** (garden rolls) or the **Cha Gio** (spring rolls). Like many of our better area Vietnamese restaurants, *Café Dalat* has an excellent assortment of soups: my faves are the *very* spicy **Bun bo Hue** (beef and vermicelli noodles, topped with spring onions and cilantro), the **Pho tai nam dac-biet** (beef and rice noodle soup), and the **Pho ga** (chicken and rice noodles).

The **kho** dishes, prepared through a relatively lengthy process of simmering, are a good place to start for your entrées. The **Cari bo**, "tender" beef in a traditional curry sauce, is indeed tender and well worth trying, although it could stand a little more seasoning. For lovers of heat, try the **Ga xao**, spicy citronella chicken, citronella being the orange flavor given by the citrus rinds used in the preparation. The **Grilled Five-Spice Pork** is also a worthy choice. The specialties of the house (as opposed to the nightly specials, which often are seafood and are usually excellent) are the flounder (either steamed or fried), or the **Banh khoai**, which is shrimp, chicken, bean sprouts, and onions, topped with a mild peanut sauce and wrapped in what they call a crepe, but is much more like a rice flour tortilla shell.

On the cooler side, try the **Mi tom**, sautéed shrimp and soft noodles, or any of the **Bun** dishes (grilled lemon chicken, grilled vegetables, grilled pork). In fact, the chef here is among the very best at this Bun thing, so if you like grilled Vietnamese fare, get thee to this particular Bunnery! The **fried rice dishes**, particularly the **Com chien bo** (sliced beef over fried rice), are also good selections.

For the money, it's hard to find a better deal, even in Arlington's increasingly-crowded Little Vietnam.

CAFÉ SAIGON

1135 N. Highland St., Arlington, VA (703/243-6522). **Nearest Metro:** Clarendon on the Orange Line. Hours: Sun.-Th, 10:00 am - 10:00 pm; F-Sat., 10:00 am - 11:00 pm. **Credit Cards:** AE, MC, V. **Price:** INEXPENSIVE.

If you know you only want delicious Vietnamese soup, go to Pho 75 down the road. But if you want an extensive selection of great soups *and* the rest of the meal too, come to **Café Sagion**. The size and quality of the menu outsrips the size and decor of the room, but you'll get some of the heartiest broth dishes around plus a number of first-rate appetizers and entrées.

You've got 12 soups to choose from, with a broader selection than anywhere else (Pho 75 only has variations on *pho*, the beef noodle soup). The best of what is a very good lot are the **Hanoi Beef Noodle Soup (Pho Nho)**; the **Special Hue Spicy Beef Noodle Soup (Bun Bo Hue)**; **Roasted Pork and Shrimp Noodles**; and the **Seafood Yellow Noodle Soup** (which comes with shrimp, scallops, fishballs, and squid). If you're not in the mood for a soup, you may want to start with the **Saigon Special Shrimp Cake (Banh Cong)**, which is special indeed, or the **Shrimp Salad (Goi Tom)**.

If you like that caramel flavoring beloved by Vietnamese chefs, try the **Caramel Pork with Black Pepper (Thit Heo Kho Tieu)**. A tasty chicken dish is the **Grilled Chicken (Bun Ga Chanh)** with lemon peel on skewers, served over rice vermicelli.

For beef, the **Beef Wrapped in Grape Leaves (Bo La)** is excellent, a grilled beef dish cooked in wine, chopped onions, and traditional spices; another favorite is the simple **Beef Sauteed with Soft Yellow Noodles (Bo Xao Mi Mem)**. For the saefood lover, the **Whole Fresh Flounder** is a great choice, deep-fried in a ginger sauce, as is the **Butterfly Jumbo Shrimp (Tom Lan Bot)**, jumbo shrimp cooked in their "special batter" (fish sauce in a rice batter) and deep-fried. There are also three vegetarian dishes, which are adequate but not outstanding.

So if you're looking for a large selection of delicious soups and a nice variety of good Vietnamese dishes - all at a most reasonable price - you've come to the right place when you step into **Café Sagion**.

LITTLE VIET GARDEN

3012 Wilson Blvd., Arlington, VA (703/522-9686). **Nearest Metro:** Clarendon on the Orange Line. **Hours:** M-F, 10:30 am - 10:30 pm; Sat.Sun., 5:00 pm - 10:30 pm. **Credit Cards:** CB, DC, DV, MC, V. **Price:** MODERATE.

Located in the heart of Little Vietnam along scenic Wilson Boulevard, **Little Viet Garden** is one of the many inexpensive Vietnamese gems that dot the northern Virginia landscape. As is common in many of these fine establishments, atmosphere and decor are not their strong points. But the food is very good, and the price is right.

The **Spring Rolls** are crunchy but only adequate. The **Pho** (beef noodle soup) is much better. For entrées, the **Viet Garden Steak (Shaking Beef)** is a big hit with me. It's marinated in a wine sauce with garlic and butter, served on a leaf of lettuce with sautéed onions and — since this is Washington and not Hanoi — an Idaho spud (well, some kind of fried potato). The noodle and vermicelli dishes are quite good; my favorite is the **Viet Garden Crispy Noodles**. Unlike some other joints, the noodles truly are crispy here, and the chicken, beef, shrimp, scallops and vegetables are cooked in a brown sauce that has some real character.

The **Grilled Lemon Grass Pork on Skewers with Rice Vermicelli** is a good representative dish if you're into vermicelli (long, thin white thread-like noodles) — which you should be! But any of the noodle dishes will do; they're all good here. Other house specials I'd recommend are the **Golden Pancake**, a crepe filled with bean sprouts, chicken, and shrimp, to be eaten with green leaf, mint leaves, and mung bean, and the **Grilled Beef Wrapped with Vine Leaves** (beef marinated in their "special" sauce, served with onions, wrapped in vine leaves and grilled; it's served with green leaf and peanut sauce). For the no-beef crowd, there are three vegetarian specials, two of which are variations on fried tofu.

While it's hard to be romantic with traffic whizzing by, there is live music and an outdoor cafe when the weather turns decent. If you want a bigger and better selection of pho and other soups, go around the corner to Café Saigon or south a mile or two to Pho 75. But if you want good grilled fare and tasty noodle dishes, try **Little Viet Garden**.

NAM'S

111220 Georgia Ave., Wheaton, MD (301/933-2525). **Nearest Metro:** Wheaton on the Red Line. **Hours:** T-F, 11:00 am - 3:00 pm, 5:00 pm - 9:30pm; F, 11:00 am - 3:00 pm, 5:00 pm - 10:30pm; Sat.-Sun., 11:00 am - 10:30 pm; closed M. **Credit Cards:** AE, MC, V. **Price:** INEXPENSIVE.

Nam's is one of Wheaton's growing coterie of top-notch ethnic eateries. The chef here taught the chef at downtown's classy **Saigonnais** restaurant, and if you're familiar with their bill of fare, you know that you're getting Vietnamese dining at its finest. Set in a little strip mall onGeorgia Ave., **Nam's** is small and somewhat crowded, with no atmosphere to speak of at all - but the food is great!

To start with, in addition to the justly popular **Spring Rolls (Cha Gio)**, ground pork, crab meat, shrimp, vermicelli, and onions wrapped in rice paper and fried, consider ordering the **Shredded Pork Skin Rolls (Bi Cuon)**, thin rice paper wrapped around shredded pork skin, vermicelli, and vegetables, and the **Shrimp on Sugar Cane (Chao Tom)**, grilled sugar cane coated with shrimp paste, garlic, and *nuoc mam* (fish sauce). Many of the best dishes here seem to favor the use of this sauce. The **Seafood Noodles Soup (Mi Hai San)** is a clear soup with shrimp, crab meat, fish, squid, and egg rice noodles; the classic **Hanoi Beef Soup (Pho)** is a beef broth with sliced beef and rice noodles. Both are superior versions of these common soups.

For entrées, my picks are the **Grilled Pork on Rice Crepe**, a simple but delicious Saigon specialty of sliced marinated pork with *nuoc mam*, garlic, lemon grass, served over soft rice crepes; the **Ginger Chicken (Ga Kho Gung)**, marinated chicken cooked in *nuoc mam* and fresh ginger root; the **Hanoi Beef Saute (Bo Xao Chua)**, sautéed tender beef cooked with cucumber, pineapple, tomato, and onion; the **Grilled Beef on Soft Rice Stick (Banh Hoi Bo Nuong Sa)**, grilled marinated beef, topped with sesame seeds and served over thin vermicelli; and, last but certainly not least, the **Shrimp Hue Style (Tom Kho Hue)**, which combines nice-sized shrimp with pork slices, cooked in a hot pepper-based sauce.

Desserts, like the flambés and flan, are good but pretty sweet, so watch out. **Nam's** keeps getting better and better, so without hesitation I can tell you you're going to be treated to one swell Vietnamese meal.

NAM VIET

1127 N. Hudson St., Arlington, VA (703/522-7110). **Nearest Metro:** Clarendon on the Orange Line. **Hours:** 10:00 am - 10:00 pm, daily. **Credit Cards:** AE, MC, V. **Price:** INEXPENSIVE.

Early to rise seems to be the **Nam Viet** philosophy; they open at 10:00 am, so if you've got a craving for morning spring rolls or jasmine rice, this is the place for you. But whenever you come, you'll get a quality meal and you won't pay a lot for it.

These folks really perservere too. Last time I wandered in, an area blackout had other restaurants closed or in a heavy tizzy; **Nam Viet's** staff didn't blink an eye and dinner proceeded more romantically under candle-power. The menu is huge, but let me pick out a few classics and urge you to experiment beyond these meager samplings.

On the appetizer front, the **Crispy Rolls (Cha Gio)** are sometimes on the greasy side, but nicely seasoned. But the soups are excellent choices here; I particularly like the **Special Hue Spicy Beef with Noodle Soup (Bun Bo Hue)**, which, true to its name, is indeed a spicy beef broth that will have you, after you're done, asking yourself why you ordered anything else.

Of all the pork dishes, I'd recommend the **Caramel Pork with Black Pepper (Thit Heo Kho Tieu)**, pork coated in caramel and grilled with a generous amount of pepper. For chicken, go with the mildly spicy **Curried Chicken (Cari Ga)**, served with coconut milk, or the **Roasted Quail (Com Chim Cut)** with steamed jasmine rice. The best beef dish is the **Nam Viet Special Beef (Bo Dum La)**, a delicious wrapped beef dish stuffed with bean, vermicelli, mushrooms, and onions, cooked in wine, fish sauce, and other Vietnamese seasonings. The fried rice and vegetarian specials are rather plain, but perfectly good choices.

The owner is a friendly fellow who takes care that his food is high quality and that his customers are happy. He scores well on both counts.

PHO 75

Three Locations: 1711 Wilson Blvd., Arlington, VA (703/525-7355). **Nearest Metro:** Court House on the Orange Line; 1510 University Blvd. East, Langley Park, MD (301/434-7844). **Nearest Metro:** N/A; and 3103 Graham Road, Suite B, Falls Church, VA (703/204-1490). **Nearest Metro:** N/A. **Hours for all three:** 9:00 am - 8:00 pm, daily. **Credit Cards:** None. **Price:** INEXPENSIVE.

If you've ever wanted to start off your day with a savory bowl of beef noodle soup, or any other kind of *pho*, you've come to the right place. **Pho 75** has the best Vietnamese soups in the area, bar none, and there are now a number of other places that are very good. Where else can you get 16 varieties of this kind of soup?

Set up with long tables, the inside looks more like a cafeteria than the home of the best *pho* this side of Hanoi. All the soups are cooked with rice noodles, bean sprouts, hot peppers (you can ask them to cool it on the hot stuff), lemon slices, and fresh mint leaves. You've got two sizes to choose from, a large bowl or a regular bowl, although the regular is only a wee bit smaller than the large, so for $4.95 you can be a sport and splurge already.

All the soups are delicious, although I confess to eating around the "bible tripe" in those soups that include it. Most of the soups are a variation on the **Tai, Chin, Nam, Gan, Sach** *pho*, which has slices of eye-of-round steak, well-done brisket and flank, soft tendon, and the infamous bible tripe. Most of the other soups have some of these ingredients removed, or mixed in several different combinations. If you're partial to onions, try the **Hanh dam**, a side dish of jumbo onion dipped in vinegar, for use in your *pho*. Tableside, you've got two sauces to add for flavoring, a hot red chili-based sauce and a milder plum sauce.

There is also a wide selection of drinks - 16, to be exact - the likes of which include **Xi Muoi**, iced salty plum, **Sua Dau Nanh**, soy bean milk, and **Nhan Nhuc**, dried longan berries in an icy syrup. Needless to say, sweet only begins to describe the taste. Desserts are variations on a rice pudding theme, although I am partial to **Che Tao Soan**, a green bean-based pudding of sorts.

Whether you need to warm up on a cold winter night, or are just in the mood for an unadorned Vietnamese taste treat, do yourself a favor and try **Pho 75**.

SAIGONNAIS

2307 18th Street, NW, Washington (202/232-5300). **Nearest Metro:** Dupont Circle on the Red Line. **Hours:** Lunch, 11:30 am-3:00 pm, M-F; Dinner, 5:30 pm-11:00 pm, daily. **Credit Cards:** AE, CB, DC, DV, MC, V. **Price:** MODERATE.

Saigonnais does not have a lot of room, but it does have a lot of class. It's easily the best gourmet Vietnamese place in town, even though it's occasionally inconsistent, particularly with respect to the daily specials. Still, **Saigonnais** offers elegant dishes for a reasonable sum of money.

Unlike a lot of Vietnamese restaurants, the crisp **Garden Roll** appetizer (served at room temperature) is a good choice; it's not soggy or tasteless. The **Cha Gio (Spring Roll)** is even better; it's not greasy at all. The **Shrimp on Sugar Cane** is another choice appetizer.

The entrées are usually quite good, although the occasional specialty may let you down (the **Ginger Duck** special is rather bland). But try some of their standards and you won't go wrong: any of the lemon grass dishes (your choice of pork, chicken, or beef) are all very good.

The **Grilled Shrimp and Scallops** over rice vermicelli is a also a good choice if you like seafood. Both noodle dishes are excellent (**Crispy Fried Egg Noodles** and **Pan-Fried Soft Rice Noodles**, each with beef, chicken, shrimp, scallop and assorted veggies). The **Golden Coins** is another great dish here, pork and chicken marinated in soy sauce and wine with grilled green peppers, onion, tomato, and pineapple.

One of the nicest things about **Saigonnais** is the owner/maitre d', who goes out of his way to make you feel you've made a wise choice by entering his establishment. He takes care that the service is courteous and capable, and, coupled with the savory cuisine, makes Saigonnais a worthy competitor for your Vietnamese culinary desires!

SAIGON GOURMET & EAST WIND

2635 Connecticut Ave., NW, Washington (202/265-1360). *Nearest Metro:* Woodley Park-Zoo on the Red Line.   Sister restaurant of **EAST WIND**, 809 King St., Old Town, Alexandria, VA (703/836-1515). *Nearest Metro:* King Street on the Blue Line. *Hours:* M-F, 11:30 am - 2:30 pm, 6:00 pm - 10:00 pm; Sat.-Sun., 6:00 - 10:00 pm. *Credit Cards:* AE, DC, MC, V. *Price:* MODERATE.

These two fine Vietnamese restaurants are reliable and consistent. They are grouped together here because they share the same owner and management; the menus are identical except for a few dishes.

For appetizers, the **Spring Rolls** (Cha Gio) are a good choice, better than the **Garden Rolls**. The **Shrimp Toast** is excellent, as are the soups, especially the **Beef Noodle Soup** (pho).

For entrées, the **Cinnamon Beef** is usually quite good, although it can be dry on occasion. The **Shrimp Saigon Style** is excellent, with a moderately spicy sauce, with the shrimp arranged around pieces of grilled pork. I should note here that *East Wind* has a few dishes that Saigon Gourmet does not, such as the tasty **Shrimp in Crab Claw**.

Other winners here are the **Golden Coins**, a grilled pork dish in a mild brown sauce with fruit and vegetables, like pineapples, tomatoes, and onions; and the **Bo Dun**, a marinated beef tenderloin dish rolled in onions and broiled on skewers.

A nice touch here is the complimentary **Hazelnut Frangelica** served after dinner. Desserts are standard fare, although I would recommend the flan, better than many others at local Vietnamese restaurants. Overall, I think you'll enjoy *Saigon Gourmet* and *East Wind*. The decor is simple and relaxed; the service is fast and courteous. Come to either restaurant for the quality and the value.

TASTE OF SAIGON

410 Hungerford Dr., Rockville, MD (301/424-7222). **Nearest Metro:** Rockville on the Red Line. **Hours:** M-Th, 11:00 am - 10:00 pm; F-Sat., 11:00 am - 11:00 pm; Sun., 11:00 am - 9:30 pm. **Credit Cards:** AE, CB, DC, DV, MC, V. **Price:** INEXPENSIVE.

Located in Rockville's Hungerford Plaza, just off Rockville Pike, **Taste of Saigon** is an impressive addition to the legion of excellent Vietnamese restaurants in our little quadrant of America. The atmosphere is très chic, a sort-of mod-neon thing, a little on the cramped side and a far cry from the humble noodle stands or simple interiors you'd find in Vietnam - but it works for me.

Start with the **Cha Gio**, crispy spring rolls that seem to float free from the world of grease; or the **Black Pepper Crab**, a delicious appetizer of hard-shell crab, chopped and stir-fried in onions and a peppery sauce (not for the meek). The soups, especially the *pho's*, are great: I'd recommend the simple **Hanoi Pho**, sliced beef and rice noodles cooked in a beef broth and served with coriander and lime, but the other soups are good choices too.

You've got a big selection for your entrées. The **Ga Xao La Que** (basil chicken) and the hotter **Ga Xao Lan** (chicken in curry and coconut sauce, sautéed with onions and cellophane noodles) won't disappoint. Neither will the **Tom Rim**, caramel shrimp. But I'd shy away from the **Crab Cakes** and other non-Vietnamese standards, like the **Beef Burgundy** (what the heck is this doing on the menu anyway, you might well ask?). Stick with dishes like the **Bo Kho** (Saigon Beef Stew), beef chunks simmered in chili and five-spice sauce. The ginger and pepper really comes out here, and you know you're alive when the heat kicks in.

Don't forget the noodle and rice dishes, particularly six unique dishes called **Com Tam**, or Broken Rice, which is a short grain rice made with either fish sauce (*nuoc mam*) or soy sauce. Try the **Com Tam Bi**, Broken Rice with Shredded Pork, or the **Special Broken Rice Combination** with shredded and grilled pork, shrimp, and crab cake.

Altogether, the quality is high and the price is low, a perfect recipe for repeat visits when you're in the mood for Vietnamese.

EUROPEAN

CAFÉ BERLIN

322 Massachusetts Ave., NE, Washington, DC (202/543-7656). **Nearest Metro:** Union Station on the Red Line. **Hours:** M-Th, 11:00 am - 10:00 pm; F, 11:00 am - 11:00 pm; Sat., Noon - 11:00 pm; Sun., 4:00 pm - 10:00 pm. **Credit Cards:** AE, DC, MC, V. **Price:** MODERATE.

Located two blocks from the Senate, **Café Berlin** offers good, solid German fare at reasonable prices. A Senate lunch hangout, **Café Berlin's** dinner menu is worth checking out too when you have that craving for schnitzel or bratwurst.

To begin with, try the **Kartoffel Pfannkuchen**, a classic version of potato pancakes, served with apple sauce or sour cream, or the **Pikante Goulash Suppe**, seasoned with paprika and is indeed, as the menu says, "hearty."

Lunch sandwiches are decent enough, but, other than the **German Sausage Sandwich**, which offers you a choice of bratwurst or weisswurst (a white sausage), they're not especially German. The cold entrées are much better; I'd recommend the **Deutcher Wurstsalat**, a *fleischwurst* salad with julienned onions and green peppers, served over lettuce; or the **Kalte Kassler Platte**, thinly sliced smoked pork loin, served with a delicious German potato salad.

For your entrée, I'd choose one of the following: **Wiener Schnitzel**, sautéed breaded veal cutlet topped with a lemon-anchovy garnish, and served with home fries and the vegetable of the day; **Jägerschnitzel "Cafe Berlin Art,"** sautéed pork steak topped with mildly spicy bacon and a smooth mushroom sauce, served with spaetzel (noodles); or the **Sauerbraten**, a simple but tasty dish of marinated slices of beef, served with potato dumplings and red cabbage.

The special coffees here are expensive, but if you're going to splurge, the alcoholic **Rüdesheimer Coffee** will brace you for whatever it is you're apt to face once you leave this fine establishment.

OLD EUROPE

2434 Wisconsin Ave., NW, Washington, DC (202/333-7600). **Nearest Metro:** N/A. **Hours:** M-Th, 11:30 am - 3:00 pm, 5:00 pm - 10:00 pm; F-Sat., 11:30 am - 3:00 pm, 5:00 pm - 11:00 pm; Sun., 4:30 pm - 10:00 pm. **Credit Cards:** AE, DC, MC, V. **Price:** MODERATE.

For years I wandered past **Old Europe**, figuring that such heavy food was for the birds. When I finally tried this old standby, I was pleasantly surprised by the high quality and relative lightness of the fare.

Good German beer is plentiful here, served in a full-sized stein. After you've quaffed some, you may want to start with one of the soups. My favorite is their **Original Ochsenschwanzsuppe**, which is much easier to drink than to say; you know it as ox-tail soup. Or start with one of the appetizers, such as the **Alsätian Style Sausage Salad** (sliced *fleischwurst*, onions, peppers, and Swiss Cheese, mixed in a sweet and sour dressing) or the **Home Cured Graved Salmon**, prepared in a dill mustard sauce and served with toast

For the main course, you've got a big selection from which to choose. My favorites are the **Kassler Rippenspeer**, smoked loin of pork served with sauerkraut and potato dumplings; the **Kalbssteak Jäger Art**, prime veal cooked "Hunter Style," with mushrooms in a brown "rahm" sauce (heavy cream), served with spaetzel (buttery curled noodles); the **Zwiebel-Rostbraten**, a rib steak topped with roasted onions and served with home-fried potatoes and vegetables; and the cream of the crop, the **Schnitzel Old Europe**, a delicious veal dish ina light cream sauce.

Don't walk out of this place without ordering dessert. The specialty coffees are excellent, particularly the **Rüdesheimer Coffee**, made with Alsbach Brandy, Whipped Cream, and Chocolate Sprinkles. The apple pie and apple strudel are great, but you've got to try their **Schwarzwälder Kirschtorte**, the classic Black Forest Cake, made with real whipped cream, shaved chocolate, and sprinkled with Kirschwasser.

TAVERNA CRETEKOU

818 King St., Alexandria, VA (703/548-8688). *Nearest Metro:* King Street on the Blue Line. *Hours:* T-F, 11:30 am - 2:30 pm, 5:00 pm - 10:30 pm; Sat., Noon - 11:00 pm; Sun., 11:00 am - 2:30 pm, 5:00 pm - 9:30 pm. *Credit Cards:* AE, CB, DC, MC, V. *Price:* MODERATE.

Maybe I'm just a wee bit too picky about my Greek restaurants, but I have not found too many that even come close to the two listed in this book, especially *Taverna Cretekou* in Old Town Alexandria. It's not cheap, but it remains a good value considering the high quality of the food served. My only complaint relates to the service, which is always friendly but sometimesa bit slow.

Start with the **Saganaki Me Garides** from Thessaloniki in northern Greece; it's sautéed feta cheese, crispy hot and served with shrimp and lemon, or the **Imam Baildi** from Smyrna in eastern Greece; it's baby eggplant stuffed with tomatoes, onion, pine nuts, and raisins - sweet, salty, and nutty tastes blended together in a delicious cold appetizer. It's different enough from the Turkish dish of the same name that you should compare and contrast; I like both versions a lot.

The salads are wonderful at *Taverna*; my favorite is the **Fasolakia**, string beans sautéed in fresh dill, onion, garlic, and tomato. The best entrée include **Dolmades Byzantine**, rolled grape leaves filled with feta cheese, shrimp, mint, and a wild rice mixture, topped with *avgolemono* sauce, which is made with chicken stock and lemon juice; the **Exohikon**, from Crete, lamb chunks cooked with vegetables and pine nuts, wrapped in a baked filo; the **Moussaka**, also from Crete, layers of ground sirloin and eggplant in a bechamel sauce; and **Arni Psito**, roast leg of lamb seasoned with oregano and garlic. There's a substantial Greek wine list of both red and white that you may want to experiment with as well.

How sweet do you like your dessert? If you're prepared to pay the price, try the sinful **Kadaifi**, a savory shredded filo pastry filled with walnuts and almonds, and topped with honey and cinnamon. *Taverna Cretekou* prepares consistently good Greek food for good value.

YANNI'S

3500 Connecticut Ave., NW, Washington, DC (202/362-8871). **Nearest Metro:** Cleveland Park on the Red Line. **Hours:** Sun.-Th 11:30 am - 10:30 pm; F-Sat., 11:30 am - 11:00 pm. **Credit Cards:** AE, MC, V. **Price:** MODERATE.

Yanni's is a newcomer to DC, and not too soon for me. The way I see it, there are precious few good Greek restaurants in this area, and any good or great ones are welcome. The room is small and somewhat crowded, but Yanni's features very good Greek cuisine.

Cold appetizers you should consider are the **Tzatziki**, a mixture of yogurt, thinly-sliced cucumbers, garlic, and Greek herbs; dip it in pita bread and you've got a new snack food you'll want to recreate at home! The **Eggplant Melitzanosalata** is a smoked "mousse" of whipped eggplant, garlic, olive oil, lemon juice, and herbs, also designed to be dipped in pita. For cold appetizers, the best of a good lot is the **Spanakopita**, a delicious flaky layered filo with spinach and feta cheese.

The **Souvlaki** choices are great; charbroiled and tender chicken or beef. The **Baked Pastichio** (pronounced pas-teetz-io), served in a deep dish with several layers of pasta, meat, spices, tomato, eggs, and bechamel sauce (a creamy milk and flour sauce), ought to be on your list here, as should the **Mousaka Plaka**, a great mousaka dish with sliced potatoes, eggplant, zucchini, and ground beef topped with bechamel sauce. And if you don't fancy **Octopus**, which you can get charbroiled here, try the non-greasy **Kalamarakia**, a Greek variant of calamari (fried, crispy baby squid).

Desserts are homemade, and, while suffering from the same excessive sweetness that ethnic restaurants can't seem to get enough of, the **Baklava** here is terrific, made with a fine filo, crushed nuts, and "pure Greek honey." If you like Greek food, come to **Yanni's**.

BEDUCI

2014 P St., NW, Washington, DC (202/467-4466). **Nearest Metro:** Dupont Circle on the Red Line. **Hours:** Lunch, M-F, 11:30 am - 2:30 pm; Dinner, M-Th, 5:30 pm - 10:00 pm; F-Sat., 5:30 pm - 10:30 pm, Sun., 5:00 pm - 9:00 pm. **Credit Cards:** AE, CB, DC, DV, MC, V. **Price:** EXPENSIVE.

The Italian-sounding name **BeDuCi** is owner Jean-Claude Garrat's attempt at creating a neighborhood acronym equal to New York's "Tribeca" or "SoHo," the name representing the words "Below Dupont Circle." The interior decor is Mediterranean: light and airy with whitewashed walls and some interesting black-and-white photos on the walls sporting a North African motif.

First, a word on the daily specials: there's quite a few of them, and most are excellent. As for the permanent menu, I like the **Chiffonade of Carpaccio, Prosciutto, and Smoked Salmon**, a delicious cold appetizer of thinly sliced steak, cured ham, and salmon, served with mustard and apple horseradish. The **Pantelleria Grilled Merguez** (mildly spicy beef and lamb sausages served over polenta - yellow cornmeal - with tomato sauce) and the **Robertel Portabello Mushrooms** (grilled oversized portabello mushrooms marinated in olive oil, herbs, and vinegar) are the way to go in the hot appetizer department; for soup, the **Chilled Creamy Gazpacho**, a bit on the heavy side, is nevertheless delectable, with pieces of lobster and asparagus.

For pasta entrées, I'd stay away from the **Ravioli Di Spinaci** (ravioli filled with spinach and ricotta cheese), because the sage-butter sauce is too watery. But the **Gnocchi Al Capperi Spinaci** (potato dumplings covered in a great tomato sauce, with capers, leaf spinach, and black olives) and **Penne Di Dadini Di Pollo** (short pasta with diced chicken, peas, and ham in the same great tomato sauce) are the pasta champions here. Other superb entrées include the **Jozale Fish of the Day**, steamed with sweet garlic and zucchini and served over couscous; and the **Betsinart Grilled Veal**, which is a grilled veal scaloppini, covered with herbed oil. Even at some of the best Italian restaurants, the house red wine is usually pretty mediocre. Not so here; try the Moreno *Montepulciano d'abruzzo* for one of the smoothest semi-dry Italian wines that has ever masqueraded as a mere house wine.

For desserts, you'd be one insaniac not to try the **Chocolate Indulgence Cake** or the **Strawberries Cassis or Zabaglione**. And while I'd be surprised if the acronym sticks to the area, I think **BeDuCi** will be around for some time to come.

BICE

601 Pennsylvania Ave., NW, Washington (202/638-2423). NOTE: Entrance on Indiana Ave. **Nearest Metro:** National Archives on the Yellow Line. **Hours:** M-Th, 11:30 am - 3:00 pm, 5:30 pm - 10:30 pm; F,11:30 am - 3:00 pm, 5:30 pm - 11:30 pm; Sat., 5:30 pm - 11:30 pm. **Credit Cards:** AE, CB, DC, MC, V. **Price:** EXPENSIVE.

Bice has been bringing fine, fancy Italian food to Americans since 1926, but only recently in Washington. Located just a few blocks from the Capitol, Bice is an elegantly furnished, modern ristorante, with gentlemen expected to wear jacket and tie and where waiters are frocked in what looks like a white lab coat. But, as with most things elegant, there is a price to pay, and this one is pretty hefty.

The salads and appetizers are uniformly good, but the best are the **Insalata Caprese** with tomatoes, olive oil, fresh mozzarella, and basil; and the **Grilled Sausage** with braised white beans and polenta (corn meal). The multigrain nutted bread served before dinner and the **Pellegrino water** are both nice touches. But strangely enough, the salads don't come with salad forks and there are no bread plates.

For grilled entrées, try the roasted lamb or one of their veal dishes, particularly the **Breaded Veal Chop Milanese Style**, which is a large affair pounded flat and delicately seasoned. The **Roasted Pheasant** with spinach and onions is not greasy or overly gamey, as is often the case in other establishments. There is usually a good selection of fresh seafood from which to choose, but I would stick with one of their meat or pasta dishes. For the latter, one of their better choices is the **Pennette Alla Arabiata**, which is penne pasta cooked in a fantastic spicy tomato sauce. For those who don't usually believe the menu when it says hot, this time it's true! Stay away from the **Jumbo Lump Crab Meat**; you've had better elsewhere. But the **Tagliolini** pasta with shrimp, asparagus and sliced tomato is out of this world.

Desserts are rich and creamy. The **Crema Catalana** (creme brulée) is a good rendition of this old favorite. The **Sfogliatina d'albicochhe**, apricots and vanilla cream in a puff pastry, and **Strawberry Rhubarb** are two other dessert winners. As a pricey place, *Bice* does a number of things better than most, but you can get great Italian food at other restaurants for less cash.

GALILEO

1120 21st St., NW, Washington, DC (202/293-7191). **Nearest Metro:** Farragut North on the Red Line. **Hours:** M-Th, 11:30 am - 2:00 pm, 5:30 pm - 10: pm; F, 11:30 am - 2:00 pm, 5:30 pm - 10:30 pm; Sat., 5:30 pm - 10:30 pm; Sun., 5:00 pm - 9:30 pm. **Credit Cards:** AE, CB, DC, DV, MC, V. **Price:** EXPENSIVE.

This is a hard place to review; the menu turns over daily. One thing never changes: the exceptional quality of the food, with occasional lapses. The out-of-this-world gastronomic quality matches the astronomic prices, but it's a meal you won't soon forget.

There are a number of repeat dishes, or at least there are a number I seem to see when I slip in. From the *antipasti* menu, some of the sensational appetizers here are **Peperoni Marinati**, marinated roasted peppers with garlic, basil, olive oil, and black olives; the **Insalata di Asparagi con Tartuo Nero**, a wonderful asparagus salad with a uniquely delicious black truffle sauce; and the **Testa di Portobello**, grilled oversized portobello mushrooms with parsley, olive oil, and one of my favorite spices, sweet garlic cloves. The texture and preparation of these *antipasti* are hard to find elsewhere; the breads are homemade and fresh as can be.

The pasta and grilled dishes at **Galileo** are about as perfect as you can get, with some notable exceptions: I have never been satisfied with their **risottos** and, at either $25 or $45 a pop, they had better shine. Stay instead with the **fettucine, tagliatella**, or **pappardelle**; recently they had a pappardelle (a wide, flat pasta) with sausage and pepper in a beautifully-spiced tomato sauce. Grilled seafood is always cooked with Italian herbs, lemon juice, and olive oil, and, while not as strong as the pastas, are often terrific.

Grilled meats are excellent; chicken breast and baby pheasant dishes are usually creative and tender, but the all-time winner for me is their **Costoletta di Vitello Marinata**, a rib rack of lamb marinated in rosemary, olive oil, sage, wild mushrooms, and glazed in a veal stock. Words fail!

Here is one place you'll want to save room for dessert; they are among the best final courses you'll find anywhere. Oft-served dessert champs are fruits like strawberries, blackberries, raspberries, and blueberries topped with *zabaglione* cream, and the **Tiarami Su**, a variation on the classic served with mascarpone mousse and lady fingers dipped in espresso. Put that diet on hold, forget about the rent this month, and have a consummate Italian feast at **Galileo.**

I MATTI

2436 18th St., NW, Washington, DC (202/462-8844). **Nearest Metro:** Dupont Circle on the Red Line. **Hours:** M-Th, Noon - 11:00 pm; F-Sat., Noon - 11:30 pm; Sun., 11:30 am - 10:00 pm. **Credit Cards:** AE, CB, DC, MC, V. **Price:** MODERATE.

Let me start off by saying that **I Matti** is the best Italian value in town. The food is usually excellent, the service expert (particularly with regard to wine assistance) and friendly. The hardwood floors and tasteful decor make this place a joy to dine in, and the room is not so small that you feel crowded.

The menu changes every few weeks, but most items remain in one form or another. Starting with your *antipasti*, I've never been disappointed by the **Involtini de Melanzane**, grilled eggplant marinated in balsamic vinegar, nor by the **Bruschetta al Gorgonzola e Noci con Pancetta**, grilled bread topped with gorgonzola, walnuts, and pancetta. There are also some choice pizzas you may want to think about for an appetizer; my pick here is the **Pizza Margherita**, a crusty little thing with tomatoes, mozzarella, basil, and garlic.

Pasta is king here, although the grilled beef and stew dishes are close contenders. I especially like the **Maccheroncini al Peperone e Pomodoro**, a modestly-sized (but not modest tasting) pasta cooked in a terrific sauce of tomatoes, olive oil, and sweet red peppers, and the **Stracci e Pesci**, square-shaped green pasta in a shrimp/artichoke/pancetta/tomato sauce. Neither of these appear on too many other menus in this form; they are fantastic here!

The **Salsicce di Maiale ai Ferri**, grilled sausages with parmesan cheese and polenta, and the **Agnello alle Olive**, thinly-sliced lamb sautéed with hot red peppers, oregano, lemon juice, and olives, are both great ways to go in the beef department. The stews are also well worth ordering; a recent lightly spiced veal stew in a delicate tomato broth is exactly how stews should taste: not too heavy, not too much liquid, great seasoning.

Homemade desserts, served on a rolling trolley, are usually close to perfect; coffees are always good. **I Matti** should be on your "A" List of wonderful ethnic restaurants.

I RICCHI

1220 19th St., NW, Washington, DC (202/835-0459). **Nearest Metro:** Farragut North on the Red Line. **Hours:** M-F, 11:30 am - 2:30 pm, 5:30 pm - 10:30 pm; Sat., 5:30 pm - 10:30 pm; closed Sun. **Credit Cards:** AE, CB, DC, MC, V. **Price:** EXPENSIVE.

i Ricchi is one of the finest Italian restaurants in Washington, but be prepared to shell out some serious bucks. My advice: get a lobbyist to take you here. If that can't be arranged, go anyway, sit back, and enjoy a great repast, served in an elegant setting of soft comfortable chairs and a large blazing wood-burning oven.

Impressive appetizers include the **Insalata col Caprino**, warm goat cheese and mixed greens served with a balsamic vinaigrette, and the **Fettunta coi Fagioli o Pomodoro**, grilled garlic bread topped with white beans or diced tomatoes and fresh basil. And try the **Ribollita**, a delicious thick Tuscan soup of thick vegetables and bread.

The pasta entrées are the strongest; they're creative, homemade and therefore always fresh. Two of my favorites are the **Tortelloni al Burro**, tortelloni filled with ricotta and spinach, served with sage butter or a tomato and cream sauce; and the **Spaghettini Mare e Monti**, thin spaghetti, shrimp, and wild mushrooms in a light tomato sauce made with traditional herbs.

Their oak-fired grilled dishes are very good too. The **Spiedino Toscano** are skewers of sausage, veal, quail, and sage croutons; the sausage is made on-site and is packed with flavor! The ultra-expensive **Filetto alla Zingara** is an out-of-this-world filet of beef sautéed with roasted red peppers, mushrooms, plum tomatoes, and white truffles, served with truffled polenta (mashed cornmeal) on the side. And the **Costolette D'Agnello a Scottadito**, grilled baby lamb chops marinated in lemon and rosemary, is about the best lamb chop dish you'll ever have.

The wine list is extensive and replete with award-winning vintages and reserves. And don't forget the side dishes, cheeses, and desserts, especially the **Pecorino e Pere** (Tuscan sheep's milk cheese with pear slices). While some may question the value - and there is no doubt that some of the prices are more in line with the cost of launching NASA rockets - the quality of the food at *i Ricchi* is hard to beat.

NOTTE LUNA

809 15th St., NW, Washington (202/408-9500). *Nearest Metro:* McPherson
Square on the Blue/Orange Line. *Hours:* M-Th, 11:00 am - 11:00 pm; F, 11:00
am - Midnight; Sat., 5:00 pm - Midnight; Sun., 5:00 pm - 11:00 pm. *Credit
Cards:* AE, CB, DC, DV, MC, V. *Price:* EXPENSIVE.

This joint really hops, man. The name is Italian for something akin to
"Moonlit Night." The inside is stylish, with a chic LA or NY happening look.
The service is excellent and the waiters are knowledgeable. Ask your waiter
for wine recommendations; most know what they're talking about.

The food is nouvelle in the Cal-Ital (California-Italian) mode, but there are
some authentic Old World recipes (moderately jazzed up) that make this place
one of the best Italian restaurants in the city. And they know it - hence the
hefty price tag.

A hard garlicky **Foccacio bread** precedes the meal, accompanied by
goat's milk butter and olives. The **Tuscan Black Bean Soup** topped with sour
cream is a winner, as is the **Wild Mixed Greens w/Roasted Peppers**.

For entrées, two consistently great dishes are the **Penne** pasta, one of
their best pastas, and the **Papperdelle**, wide flat noodles in a meat and beef
ragu. The **Risotto** is very rich, but if that doesn't bother you, it's well worth
ordering. Grilled chicken and veal dishes are first-rate as well. The specials are
almost always on target, interesting and usually out of the ordinary.

Save some room for the end-game: desserts should not be missed here.
The **Warm Strawberry Rhubarb Tart** is excellent, as are the **Tira Mi Su**
(ladyfingers drenched in liqueur) and the **Chocolate Granache**. For jazzed-
up pastas, terrific Italian salads, and a hip place to dine, try *Notte Luna*

PRIMI PIATTI

Two locations: 2013 I (Eye) St., NW, Washington, DC (202/223-3600). **Nearest Metro:** Farragut West on the Blue Line; and 8045 Leesburg Pike (Rt. 7), Vienna, VA (703/893-0300). **Nearest Metro:** Vienna on the Orange Line. **For both - Hours:** M-Th, 11:30 am - 2:30 pm, 5:30 pm - 10:30 pm; F, 11:30 am - 2:30 pm, 5:30 pm - 11:30 pm; Sat., 5:30 pm - 11:30 pm; Sun., 5:30 pm - 9:30 pm. **Credit Cards:** AE, DC, MC, V. **Price:** EXPENSIVE.

Primi Piatti is one of several great downtown Italian restaurants (there is also a branch in Vienna, VA), and this place just keeps getting better and better. The decor is elegant, the service professional, and the quality deserving of the highest praise. It often gets ignored by various critics, for reasons beyond me. Sauces and cheeses are the strong points here.

You won't go wrong with any of the appetizers, so choose those that sound appealing; two of my favorites are the **Scamorza Grigliata**, grilled smoked mozzarella with grilled vegetables and olive oil; and the cold **Carpaccio di Pesce Spada**, swordfish carpaccio with diced orange and pink peppercorn, topped with olive oil and lemon.

I'm very impressed with their pastas, but I'll limit myself to three recommendations: the **Agnolotti di Ricotta e Spinaci**, stuffed pasta filled with ricotta cheese and spinach in a light cream sauce; perhaps the best penne dish in town, the **Penne con Salsa di Pomodori Secchi e Formaggio Caprino** (short flat pasta cooked with sun-dried tomatoes and goat cheese sauce); and the **Fettucine di Pomodoro**, a tomato fettucine with artichokes and mascarpone cheese sauce. There are also six fancy pizzas to choose from, baked in their wood-burning oven.

Consider also their **Scallopine di Salmone Ripiene**, a salmon scallopini filled with a shiitake mushroom mousse, steamed in white wine and served with diced zucchini, leeks, and carrots. The salmon is very tasty in this special mousse. Grilled dishes are good but not their strongest suit; in this area though I like the **Petto di Anatra Alla Griglia**, a relatively unfatty grilled duck breast cooked with raspberry vinegar and juniper berries sauce, served with grilled polenta (corn meal).

Settle back with some excellent espresso or cappuccino, pick a dessert that strikes your fancy, and feel complacent in the knowledge that you have just experienced a delightful gourmet Italian meal.

SFUZZI

Union Station, NW, Washington, DC (202/842-4141). *Nearest Metro:* Union Station on the Red Line. *Hours:* 11:30 am - 2:00 pm, daily; T-F, 6:00 pm - 10:00 pm. *Credit Cards:* AE, DC, MC, V. *Price:* HIGH MODERATE.

Sfuzzi (pronounced Foo-zi) is known to many as a pricey lunch place, but it's also a dinner place - where the prices are more in line with other good Italian restaurants. This sleek, hip place offers some of the more interesting Italian food you'll get in this city.

Don't fill up on the freshly baked breads, served with an olive oil dipping sauce that is sure to send your cholesterol through the roof. For appetizers, I find the **Fried Calimari** nothing special, but the **Roasted Portabello Mushrooms and Asparagus** with tomato vinaigrette is much better. The **Mozzarella and Beefsteak Tomatoes** salad is excellent, served with roasted peppers and pesto.

The pizzas are also a good deal here. One of the more unusual but fun pizzas is the **Smoked Chicken with Carmelized Onions, Goat Cheese, and Rosemary**. For other entrées, the pastas are usually on target. My favorites in this category are the **Rigatoni** served with sweet sausage, green peppers, mozzarella, and oregano; and the **Penne with Grilled Chicken** served with wild mushrooms, thyme, and romano cheese. From their specialty list, I like the **Romano Crusted Chicken Breast** with Roma Tomato Basil Sauce, served over linguini; and the **Marinated Grilled Shrimp**, cooked in lemon, garlic, and saffron.

The next time you have an errand to run at Union Station, and find yourself there around lunch or dinner, don't go to the crowded food court downstairs. Visit *Sfuzzi* instead for a fine Italian repast.

TRATTÚ

1823 Jefferson Pl., NW, Washington, DC (202/466-4570). **Nearest Metro:** Dupont Circle on the Red Line. **Hours:** Lunch, M-F, 11:30 am - 2:30 pm; Dinner, 5:30 pm - 11:00 pm daily. **Credit Cards:** AE, CB, DC, MC, V. **Price:** MODERATE.

Trattú is a comfy little trattoria on cozy little Jefferson Place, sandwiched in between bustling Connecticut Ave. and 19th Street. A little on the understaffed side, patient diners will find the meal worth waiting for.

For the anitpasti appetizers, I'd recommend the **Bruschetta al Peperoni**, a small slab of "country" bread toasted and topped with roasted green and red peppers, garlic, and a generous helping of olive oil. Be bold and try the **Calamari Freddi**, a cold marinated squid dish on a bed of lettuce. If you prefer soup and salad to begin your meal, the **Pasta e Fagioli**, a simple bean and pasta soup, and the **Insalate di Mozzarella** (tomato and mozzarella salad) should do the trick.

The pastas are the way to go here; I'd be more selective with the meat and seafood, although there are some fine picks here too, especially the veal dishes. The **Tortellini con Salsa** is an excellent veal and pasta dish (the pasta is stuffed with vegetables); go with the tomato sauce rather than the cream sauce. The **Bucatini Amatriciana** is quite good, a thick pasta made with pieces of bacon cooked in a tomato sauce, as is the **Penne con Riccotta**, a thick pasta made with ricotta cheese and cooked in a tomato sauce. The **Capelli D'Angelo al Pesto and Marinara** is one of the better angel hair pasta dishes I've had in the area, made with basil, garlic, and pine nuts.

In the carni department (meats), try the **Vitello alla Trattú** (veal scallopini with mushrooms and peppers in a red wine sauce, or the **Saltimbocca alla Romana**, a simple veal dish with prociutto slices, served in a delicious sage and wine sauce. For seafood, go with the **Filletto di Sogliola ai Funghi** (filet of sole in a mushroom, lemon, and white wine sauce) or the **Scampi fra Diavolo** (jumbo shrimp with garlic, tomatoes, and hot peppers).

The price has climbed a bit over the years, and the wine list is not extensive, but **Trattú** remains a good value.

JALEO

480 7th St., NW, Washington, DC (202/628-7949). **Nearest Metro:** Gallery Place on the Red Line. **Hours:** Lunch, M-F, 11:30 - 2:30; Dinner, M and Sun., 5:30 - 10:00; T-Th, 5:30 - 10:30; F-S, 5:30 - 11:00. **Credit Cards:** AE, CB, DC, DV, MC, V. **Price:** MODERATE.

Jaleo is a new Spanish restaurant specializing in *tapas*, which are small dishes of various delectables, usually seasoned with garlic and olive oil. Tapas bars dot the landscape of Spain, but they are rarely spotted in the US for some unfathomable reason. I love 'em!

The thing to do here is to eyeball the menu and pick out a number of appealing cold and hot tapas. You may want to start with a soup or salad first, however; I'd recommend the **Gazpacho Andaluz**, a great gazpacho soup, or the **Ensalada de Tomate, Cebolla, y Aceitunas Negras** (whew! - tomato and onion salad with olives and thyme vinaigrette).

For the cold tapas, my picks are the **Flan de Berengena** (eggplant flan with roasted pepper sauce), the **Variedad de Embutidos** (dry cured Spanish sausages and pork tenderloin), and the **Pan con Ajo, Escalivada, y Anchoas** (roasted vegetables on garlic toast, topped with anchovies - but ask them to skip the anchovies if you're like me and not into these little critters).

The hot tapas menu is more extensive. Here I'd go with the incredible **Gambas al Ajillo**, garlic shrimp; the **Pimientos del Piquillo Rellenos de Txangurro**, sweet Spanish peppers stuffed with crab meat; the **Setas con Jerez y Queso Manchego**, wild mushrooms sautéed with sherry and Manchego cheese; and last but not least, the **Pinchito de Cantimpalitos a la Parilla**, which is none other than a skewer of grilled chorizo sausage on garlic-mashed potatoes - and if you've never had garlic-mashed potatoes, you're missing something special!

Treat yourself to one of *Jaleo's* fine dry sherries, which you can order by the glass or bottle. The sherry beautifully complements the tapas; ask the informed staff for a recommendation based on your order. If you still have room for dessert, I like the **Compota de Manzana al Pan Perdido**, an apple and bread pudding with vanilla ice cream, and the **Natilla**, a Spanish custard topped with various fruit sauces.

TABERNA DEL ALABARDERO

1776 I St., NW (entrance on 18th St.), Washington, DC (202/429-2200). **Nearest Metro:** Farragut West on the Blue/Orange Line. **Hours:** M-F, 11:30 am - 2:30 pm; Dinner, M-Th, 6:00 pm - 10:30 pm, F-Sat., 6:00 pm - 11:00 pm. **Credit Cards:** AE, CB, DC, MC, V. **Price:** EXPENSIVE.

One of four Tabernas worldwide (the other three are in Spain), Washington's **Taberna del Alabardero** is an extraordinary dining experience you'll long remember. Even though your wallet will appreciably thin out after eating here, you are getting the very best of local Spanish cuisine, served with style in elegant surroundings.

The food of three of Spain's great culinary regions is usually offered here: Cataluña, Pais Vasco, and Andalucia, sometimes on a rotating monthly basis, other times all at once. The permanent menu is small but every dish is carefully selected and prepared. The **Tapas** bar features a nice assortment for appetizers, but I'd skip those and order a few other appetizers or soup, especially the **Gazpacho Andaluz**, one of the very best around. Try the **Embutidos de España**, which are Spanish-style sausages; the **Txangurro al Graten,** Basque-style crab meat; or the **Pimientos del Piquillo rellenos**, stuffed peppers filled with shrimp, mushrooms, and spinach. When you push away the plate after this first course, you'll sigh that this is too good to be true. But there's more.

The fish of the day is always a good bet, prepared differently depending on what's being offered: sometimes it's monkfish cooked in a garlic and parsley sauce, other times grouper in a black olive sauce. The **Paella de Langosta**, a seafood and lobster paella for two, is fantastic; the spices are rich but not overwhelming. I'd also recommend **Pintada asada**, a small roasted chicken, nicely spiced and cooked in its own juices; the **Escalopines de Ternera**, stuffed veal with spinach and goat cheese; and, for something different, why not try the **Venado asado al vino de Málaga**, roasted loin of venison cooked in Málaga wine.

Desserts are rich and richly satisfying, from pears in red wine sauce to flan (Catalan cream) to chocolate mousse and more, depending on the night. One of Washington's all-around greats, **Taberna** gives you one of those great gourmet meals where you don't stagger away complaining about all the dough you've just dropped.

TERRAMAR

7800 Wisconsin Ave., Bethesda, MD (301/654-0888). **Nearest Metro:** Bethesda on the Red Line. **Hours:** T-F, 11:30 am - 2:30 pm, 5:00 pm - 10:00 pm; Sat., 5:00 - 10:00 pm; Sun., 5:00 - 9:00 pm. **Credit Cards:** AE, DV, DC, MC, V. **Price:** MODERATE.

Terramar could just as easily be listed in another part of this book, because many of the dishes are from Nicaragua, Argentina, and elsewhere in Central and South America. But the food also has a distinctive Spanish flair to it, and the extensive tapas bar forced my hand! But however you classify it, **Terramar's** Latin cooking is some of the best around town, served to you in a classy setting complete with a piazza-style fountain.

You can make a whole dinner out of tapas, of course, but I'd save myself for a few entrées. You might want to start with a soup, and if so, I'd go with the **Sopa de Frijoles Rojos**, a red bean soup topped with sour cream and *chilero*, which is a mild red chili pepper that gives the soup some zip.

The tapas choices are extensive, but on a first visit I'd recommend the **Nacatama**, a tamale done Nicaraguan-style: pork, rice, and vegetables in a steamed banana leaf; the **Vigoron**, pork, yuca, and *repollo* (cabbage to most of us); the **Alitas de Pollo**, a delicious version of peppery chicken wings, marinated in lemon and tabasco and served with sour cream; and our old friend the **Chorizo**, which serves as a reminder that simple is often best: grilled pork sausage prepared Spanish-style, served with a tortilla and *chimi-churri* (a rich dip made out of olive oil, garlic, and parsley).

For entrées, if you like steak, try the **Churrasco**. It's grilled tenderloin served with three sauces ranging from mild to hot. I also like the **Filete de Cerdo Asado** (a somewhat spicy grilled pork tenderloin marinated in lime and garlic). The seafood selection is usually first-rate; my favorites are the **Pez Espada Ranchero** (grilled swordfish steak in a spicy mixture of tomato, onion, jalapeño, and cilantro) and the **Camarones a la Parilla**, grilled shrimp cooked in your choice of two sauces: go with the garlic butter over the too-creamy jalapeño sauce.

Desserts are quite good here. Some of the entrées are priced on the high side, but the quality remains high too. All in all, a great place for sampling some fine cuisine from Spain and Latin America.

LATIN AMERICAN, CARIBBEAN, CAJUN & CREOLE

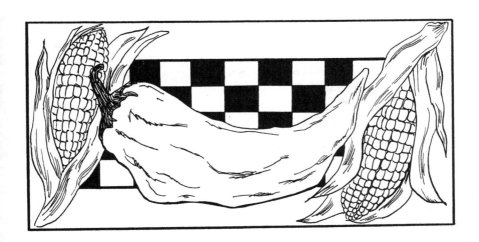

BRASIL TROPICAL

2519 Pennsylvania Ave., NW, Washington (202/293-1773). **Nearest Metro:** Foggy Bottom on the Blue Line. **Hours:** M-Th, 11:30 am - 10:00 pm; F-Sat., 11:30 am - 3:00 am; Sun. 11:30 am - 11:00 pm. **Credit Cards:** AE, DC, MC, V. **Price:** MODERATE.

Brasil Tropical seems to be the place attracting most Brazilians, a testimony either to the authenticity of the food or to the live music beginning at 10:00 on Friday and Saturday nights. On a summer eve, you can sit on their sidewalk patio and watch cars whizz by.

Seafood is the specialty here, but I've never been disappointed in other selections. Appetizers are fun here; try the **Casquinha de Siri**, crabmeat cooked in a yellow sauce of coconut milk and palm oil, mixed with chunks of green pepper, onion and tomato, served in a big clam shell. The **Camarao Tropical** is also great, shrimp sautéed with white wine, garlic and Brazilian spices. It's not spicy hot, but is powerful nonetheless.

I've had better salads and soups elsewhere, but it's hard to beat their **frutos do mar** (seafood to you and me). A classic Bahian dish called **Vatapa** is hard to get in Washington; they do it right here. It's fish and shrimp cooked in the standard sauce of coconut milk and palm oil, with peanuts, dried shrimp, onion, tomato, and green pepper. The **Camarao Presidente Fernando Collor** may be a bit out of date (Collor no longer being Brazil's El Presidente), but it's top-notch anyway: sautéed shrimp and mushrooms, flambeed in cognac and topped with a cream sauce, all served in a pineapple shell. Choose any of their **lobster** dishes and you'll be fine.

The **Feijoada**, Brazil's national specialty, is very good but not the best in town. It's a stew of black beans, dry beef, pork, and sausage, served with farofa (manioc flour fried with olive oil and onions), collard greens, orange slices, and rice. The **Brasil 2001** is a better choice (grilled beef, chicken, and pork served with collard greens, sausage, orange and fried bananas), although the beef and pork may taste a bit strange to those unaccustomed to the salty, tougher, range-fed South American beef. The chicken selection here is small, but if you're in the mood or don't like beef, try the **Frango Copacabana**, a nicely-spiced grilled chicken breast.

Desserts are nothing special here, but if you want something interesting, choose the **Romeu e Julieta**, guava paste and Brazilian cheese!

DONA FLOR

4615 Wisconsin Ave., NW, Washington (202/537-0404). **Nearest Metro:** Tenleytown on the Red Line. **Hours:** M-Th, Noon - 2:30 pm, 5:00 - 11:00 pm; F-Sun., Noon - 11:00 pm; Sat.-Sun., Brazilian brunch from Noon - 4:00 pm. **Credit Cards:** AE, CB, DC, MC, V. **Price:** MODERATE.

Dona Flor is a more staid version of the newer **Grill from Ipanema**, owned by the same people. The dining room is brightly colored, and, while not exactly festive, is nicely appointed. The menu is rife with Brazilian specialties, and is especially strong in seafood.

Start with the **Feijão**, a strongly flavored black bean soup, or the **Clams à Baiana**, a fun appetizer of clams cooked in a sauce made from coconut milk, olive oil, green peppers, and Brazilian herbs.

There is a large selection of entrées here, all served with rice and black beans, neither of which are too liquidy, as is often the case in Latin restaurants. Top seafood choices include **Bobo de Camarão**, a sautéed shrimp dish cooked in a tantalizing light cream sauce made from yuca, flour, coconut milk, peanuts, and palm oil; **Vatapá**, a Bahian specialty of fish and shrimp cooked in a blended sauce of coconut milk, crushed peanuts, palm oil, tomatoes, and Brazilian herbs; and another combo dish, the **Peixada à Brasileira**, with shrimp, mussels, clams, white fish, tomatoes, and green peppers, stewed in coconut milk.

Brazil's national dish, the **Feijoada**, has a slightly different (but still hearty) taste compared to the feijoadas made by Grill from Ipanema and Brasil Tropical; it's a stew of black beans, pork, and smoked sausage, served with collard greens, orange slices, and farofa (manioc flour fried with olive oil and onions). It's got a slightly smokier taste here, but it works for me. The chicken dishes here are all right, but I'm not wowed; I am, however, wowed by the **Churrasco Misto**, a grilled pork, chicken, and beef dish, covered with a sauce of green peppers, tomatoes, and onions, served on skewers over rice.

Dona Flor consistently delivers excellent Brazilian specialties. While the price seems to have creeped on up without a noticeable change in quality - which has always been high - it remains a Washington classic.

THE GRILL FROM IPANEMA

1858 Columbia Rd., NW, Washington (202/986-0757). **Nearest Metro:**
Dupont Circle on the Red Line. **Hours:** Sun.-Th, 6:00 pm - 11:00 pm; F-Sat.,
5:00 pm - Midnight; Sun., Noon - 4:00 pm, 5:00 pm - 11:00 pm. **Credit Cards:**
AE, DC, DV, MC, V. **Price:** MODERATE.

The decor is sharp and mod, with a metal structure against one wall
shaped like the mountains of Rio, where Ipanema summit can be found. The
newest Brazilian restaurant in Washington, it is owned by the same folks who
brought you **Dona Flor** up on Wisconsin Ave. The menus share some basic
dishes but are by no means identical. **The Grill from Ipanema** has a pretty
active bar scene, and, as befits its location in Adams Morgan, sports a younger,
hipper crowd than its sister restaurant in upper Northwest.

For appetizers, try the **Churrasquinhos**, either grilled beef, chicken or
pork served with **farofa**, which is manioc flour fried with olive oil and onions.
Or, if you like your Brazilian food on the hot side, order the **Camaroes a
Malagueta**, five spicy shrimp steamed with herbs and peppers and served
cold. The **Jacare Ao Pantanal** - fried alligator strips prepared in a honey
mustard sauce (sort of like Alligator McNuggets) - wasn't my cup of swamp
stew, but if you're feeling particularly bold you may want to do a little
experimentation. The **Caldo de Feijao** is another winner, black bean soup
with bacon and parmesan cheese served in a glass mug.

For the main event, if you like beef, come on a Wednesday or Saturday
night and have the **Feijoada**, a delicious stew of black beans, pork and
smoked meat served with a mixture of garlicky collard greens, orange slices
to absorb the rich stew, and **farofa**. This is a Brazilian specialty, originating
in northeastern Brazil, as are most other dishes on this (and most other
Brazilian restaurant) in this country.

The **Carne De Sol** is great: long thin strips of steak served with rice,
blackeye peas, and manioc (cassava, a large, starchy root, from which comes
such dessert faves as tapioca). If your into *aves* (birds), the **Frango Ao Alho**
is fantastic (grilled garlic chicken breast served with *feijao tropeiro*, rice and
collard greens). If your tastes run more toward seafood, try any of the
Moquecas or other "fruits of the sea." My favorite was the **Moqueca A
Capixaba Mista, Bahian style**, a stew of fish, shrimp, squid and scallops,
cooked in palm oil, coconut milk, tomato, garlic, cilantro, onion and green
pepper.

While a newcomer on the scene, **The Grill from Ipanema** gets my vote
for best Brazilian restaurant in town.

LOUISIANA EXPRESS CO.

4921 Bethesda Ave., Bethesda, MD, 301/652-6945. **Nearest Metro:** Bethesda on the Red Line. **Hours:** M-Th, 7:30 am - 10:00 pm, F- Sat., 7:30 am - 11:00 pm; Sun., 9:00 am - 2:30 pm. **Credit Cards:** MC, V. **Price:** MODERATE.

Picture yourself at Mardi Gras, falling down every 15 minutes from too much debauchery and drink, with wild party floats and out-of-control college co-eds shrieking and smoking, and ... and the picture you have is the opposite of what you'll find at **Louisiana Express Co.** The wild strains of Cajun Zydeco music can be heard in the background, but otherwise the atmosphere is staid and relaxed. The fluorescent lights are a bit much, the decor is on the plain side, and they could stand some additional seating. But the food is generally good, and sometimes excellent.

For starters, go with one of the **Gumbo Soups** or the **Fried Appetizers,** particularly the **Fried Shrimp Balls**. The gumbo is delicious, a little spicy but not overdone for the faint of heart. The fried appetizers are not greasy at all, and are lightly spiced.

For the main event, skip the **Etoufée,** a classic New Orleans dish featuring either chicken, shrimp, crawfish or andouille sausage (or all four mixed together in something they call **"The Works"**) in a roux sauce on a bed of white rice and scallions. I found the "cajun roux" sauce, which is a reddish brown mix of flour and butter, too heavy and on the bland side. No one can say it's too spicy. On the other hand, the **Chicken** or **Andouille Sausage Jambalaya** is great, with a little more heat than their Etouffée dishes (but again, not overpowering). Any of the **Gumbo Stews** are also a winner. If you're not worried about cholesterol or anything else of that nature, you should also consider the **Rotiserrie Chicken with Cajun Seasoning**, an excellent, moist dish, but you'll have to eat the skin since most of the flavor is to be found here. The biscuits are good, but a little doughy.

Try one of the New Orleans-style desserts, particularly the **Beignets,** which are advertised as New Orleans doughnuts but are really deep-fried dough covered with generous heapings of powdered sugar on top. The New Orleans-style **coffee** is authentic and very good, made with **chicory**, the root of a blue-flowered plant that is dried and roasted for mixing with coffee.

LULU'S NEW ORLEANS CAFE

22nd & M Streets, NW, Washington, DC (202/861-5858). *Nearest Metro:* Foggy Bottom on the Blue/Orange Line. *Hours:* M-Th, 11:30 am - 11:00 pm; F-Sat, 11:30 am - 1:00 am; Sun, 10:00 am - 4:00 pm (Jazz Brunch), 4:00 pm - 10:00 pm (Dinner). *Credit Cards:* AE, CB, DC, MC, V. *Price:* MODERATE.

Lulu's is the middle section of the Blackie's/Lulu's/Deja Vu complex, all owned by the Augur family. Lulu, wife of Blackie Augur, was the 1962 Queen of Venus, a big-time Mardi Gras Parade honor. And, while a few dishes seem to be employ Venutian recipes, overall *Lulu's* is a fun, solid Creole dining experience. The rooms are spacious, the ceilings tall, and the wrought-iron and New Orleans street signs put you in a N'awluns mood as soon as you walk through the door.

The appetizer section is ample and diverse. If you like your shrimp with their heads attached, order the **Louisiana BBQ Shrimp**, five jumbo Gulf shrimp, baked in whole butter, cracked pepper, garlic, creole spices, lemon, steak sauce and shrimp stock, with garlic bread on the side. They're good but tough; be prepared to get messy. On the other hand, the **Catfish Fingers** were bland, saved (only partly) by the Creole dipping mustard. Several good salads are on the menu here, but none are particularly Creole or Cajun. The best sandwiches are the **Cajun Po'Boy** (fried oysters served with lettuce, cabbage, and sliced tomatoes) and the **Grilled Chicken Po'Boy**.

For entrées, allow me to steer you toward the **Creole Duet in a Shell**, which is "creek shrimp" (they tasted just like regular ol' shrimp to me, but great nonetheless) and chicken cooked in a Creole sauce, served over white rice in a deep-fried tortilla shell. It's moderately spicy, but by no means too much for my weaker-kneed culinary compadres out there. Allow me to steer you away from the **Sausage and Chicken Jambalaya**, which left me cold, not a great sign for a New Orleans place. The **Seafood Gumbo** is a better choice, as is the **Flounder Moreau** (flounder stuffed with crawfish tails and blue crab meat, topped with Creole lobster sauce). The **Chicken Etoufée** is standard fare.

For dessert, try the **Creole Cream Cheese Cake** (a fairly light cheesecake smothered with caramel sauce) and the **Bread Pudding**, made the way nature intended (french bread mixed with eggs, milk, sugar. raisins and spices).

While not perfect, Lulu's has a good selection of good-to-great dishes. Ask for a little extra oomph here and you'll be okay. If you get the right thing at *Lulu's*, you'll enjoy some good Creole cooking.

RT'S

3804 Mt. Vernon Ave., Alexandria, VA (703/684-6010). *Nearest Metro:* N/A. *Hours:* M-Th, 11:00 am - 10:30 pm; F-Sat., 11:00 am - 11:00 pm; Sun., 4:00 pm - 9:30 pm. *Credit Cards:* AE, CB, DC, MC, V. *Price:* MODERATE-TO-EXPENSIVE.

RT's is a small Creole and Cajun place, offering incredible New Orleans-style dishes with a simple, unassuming flair. While occasionally off on an entrée here and there, and despite a recent upswing in prices, it's still one of my favorite restaurants and the best Cajun place around: great food, friendly service.

Start with one of these appetizers: the **Acadian Peppered Shrimp**, or the **"Jack Daniels" Shrimp with Lump Crabmeat**. Both are barbecued Cajun dishes employing the full range of Cajun spices. Be experimental and try the **Creole Alligator Stew**, which is milder than it sounds (Creole dishes are supposed to be less hot than Cajun).

The **Crawfish Etouffée** is sautéed crawfish drowned in Cajun spices, and the **Grilled Shrimp and Andouille Sausage** is a shrimp and spicy sausage combo topped with Creole mustard sauce and served on rice; both are first-rate. The **New Orleans Blackened Fish** varies day to day, but it's not let me down yet. I also strongly recommend the **Spicy Pecan Crusted Chicken**, topped with sautéed shrimp and *RT's* signature Creole mustard sauce, and the **Pasta Jambalaya**, a healthy heapin' o' penne pasta mixed with Gulf Shrimp, Andouille Sausage, spicy roast pork, and sliced chicken.

If you're looking for a place where you can get great Creole and Cajun dishes, and not just one or the other, *RT's* is the place to go. It gets my vote as the best New Orleans-style restaurant in the metropolitan area.

CAFÉ ATLANTICO

1819 Columbia Rd., NW, Washington, DC (202/328-5844). **Nearest Metro:** Dupont Circle on the Red Line. **Hours:** Sun.-W, 5:30 pm - 10:00 pm; Th, 5:30 pm - 11:00 pm; F-Sat., 5:30 pm - Midnight. Bar stays open until 3:00 am Th-Sat. **Credit Cards:** AE, MC, V. **Price:** MODERATE.

Café Atlantico has nothing to fear from the rash of new, some quite good, Caribbean joints opening up around town. For my cash, this is the one to beat. Originally a Santo Domingo (Dominican Republic) restaurant, **Café Atlantico** offers a nice mix of regional food far better than the fare you may have encountered at a typical Caribbean resort.

To begin with, you may want to order one of their expensive but powerful mixed rum drinks. When you're ready for solid sustenance, try the **Ceviche de Salmón con Aguacate**, salmon prepared with cilantro, red bell pepper, onion and scallion, marinated in lime juice and olive oil and served with avocado slices. I also like the **Pinchitos de Pollo en Tres Salsas**, chicken pieces on skewers, marinated with "Island" spices (things like bay leaves, thyme, allspice, etc.), and served in a great black bean sauce with a red pepper purée and avocado sauce. Their version of gazpacho soup (**Gazpacho Caribeño**) is made with tomato, cucumber, bell pepper, olive oil, avocado, papaya and mango, and is one of the two best gazpacho soups in Washington (the other being the Spanish restaurant Taberna del Alabardero).

One of the more unique dishes hard to find elsewhere is the delicious **Lomo de Cerdo Empanizado, Relleno de Queso y Con Salsa Curry**, which certainly is a mouthful to say, let alone eat. It's pork loin stuffed with cheese, cooked in a fairly hot curry sauce, accompanied by fried sweet plantains and a jam of sorts made out of mangoes. For seafood lovers, their **Salmón a la Parilla** and **Lubina** (stuffed bass) dishes are both excellent choices. From their grill, I highly recommend the **Pollo a la "Jerk,"** a crisp, spicy chicken breast, marinated in traditional jerk spices; and the **Solomillo de Temera Marinado en Tomillo Caribeño**, beef tenderloin marinated in a thyme and olive oil mixture and glazed with a honey-mustard sauce.

Don't forget to order a few side dishes: there are two tasty plantain dishes, a great yuca purée (**Puré de Yuca**), and the **Frijoles** (refried beans), both of which have some real character! You may not actually start planning a trip to Santo Domingo to try the real McCoy after eating here, but you'll be tempted.

HIBISCUS CAFÉ

3401 K St., NW, Washington, DC (202/338-0408). **Nearest Metro:** N/A. **Hours:** 6:00 pm - 11:00 pm daily. **Credit Cards:** AE, MC, V. **Price:** MODERATE.

Hibiscus is one of the more interesting, hip places to try some different kind of cookin.' The decor is steel, metal, and glass; there's some funky Jamaican art work on the walls, and easily the heaviest chairs I've ever encountered. The food can be excellent, but it can also be just ho-hum. And for a small place, the service leaves a lot to be desired. Still, if you're not in a hurry, it's a fun place with an interesting menu that worth exploring.

Start with the **Pumpkin Soup**, which is exactly what you'd expect: thick orange-colored pumpkin pureé. My favorite appetizers are the **Crabmeat Fritters**, which are fritters stuffed with jumbo lump crabmeat, served with a creamy ginger sauce; and the **Jerk Buffalo Wings**, which are delicious but not overly spicy, which "jerk" should be. And I don't think there are too many other places around town where you can get shark meat beignets (**Shark and Bake**).

For entrées, try the **Stuffed Boneless Chicken Breast** cooked in a ginger and mango sauce. But the **Jerked Quail**, while adequate, lacks any heat or interesting seasoning. Vegetables are pretty much missing as side dishes or accompaniments, but you can order the **Veggie Mix Up**, a smooth collection of sautéed vegetables, simmered in a curry and coconut milk sauce.

The seafood dishes, however, really shine here. The **Poached Red Snapper Fillet** comes with shrimp and is cooked in a tasty pumpkin and coconut sauce. (Pumpkins and coconuts seem to be a mainstay here!) The **Seafood Creole** could use a bit more fire, but is one of their best dishes: salmon, shrimp, and lobster in a tomato sauce, served over what they call "rasta" pasta.

For dessert, go with the **Bread Pudding**, served in a fruity plum sauce. If the service improves and the quality remains high, *Hibiscus* will be around for a long time.

LA CANTANITA

3100 Clarendon Blvd., Arlington, VA (703/524-3611). **Nearest Metro:** Clarendon on the Orange Line. **Hours:** M-F, 11:00 am - 3:00 pm, 5:30 pm - 11:00 pm; Sat., 3:00 pm - 11:00 pm; Sun., 3:00 pm - 10:00 pm. **Credit Cards:** DV, MC, V. **Price:** MODERATE.

Having moved from their rather plain digs on Wilson Blvd. across from the Ballston Common in November 1993, La Cantanita is perhaps the last remaining first-rate Cuban joint north of Miami Beach and south of the Bronx. It certainly is the best in the Washington area. The service is fast and friendly. And in their new government building location on Clarendon Blvd., they have nearly twice as much space, and a new, tropical look, with a lounge area and a private dining room.

Seafood and beef dishes are the way to go here. For appetizers, I love the **Gambas al Ajillo**, shrimp sautéed in olive oil, white wine, and garlic; it's a great combination as long as the olive oil is kept to a minimum, which they do. The **Chorizo con Queso**, Spanish sausage with melted cheese, is also wonderfully done, or the **Empanadas de Carne**, not your everyday beef empanada. Here it's made with a crispier shell and with more flavor than the usual dish in most Mexican places.

For entrées, the best here are the **Bifstec a la Criolla**, steak Cuban-style (pan-seared) with fried onions; **Porco Asado**, marinated roast pork, cooked overnight in a zippy garlic sauce; **Fiesta Marinara**, red snapper, shrimp, scallops, clams, mussels, and squid, cooked in a wine sauce with onions; and **Camarones Enchiladas**, shrimp sautéed in tomatoes and wine sauce with spices and herbs. The sauces are excellent here, the portions generous, and the rice more buttery than you might find at Mexican restaurants, which I happen to like. And if you like café au lait, the **Coffee con Leche** is a must here; three-quarters of your mug is filled with hot milk, followed by a rich aromatic coffee.

If Fidel could only taste the fruits of *La Cantanita's* free market cooking, my guess is that he'd free Cuba tomorrow. Viva the Little Canteen!

BURRITO BROTHERS

Three locations: 1524 Connecticut Avenue, NW, Washington (202/332-2308; for delivery call 546-TOGO for Dupont Circle and Capitol Hill locations). **Nearest Metro:** Dupont Circle on the Red Line. **Hours:** M-Sat, 11:00 am - 10:00 pm, Sun., 11:00 am - 8:00 pm; 3273 M Street, NW, Washington, at Potomac Street (202/965-3963; same number for delivery). **Nearest Metro:** N/A. **Hours:** Sun.-W, 11:00 am - Midnight, Th-Sat, 11:00 am - 3:00 am. **Capitol Hill**, 205 Pennsylvania Avenue, SE (202/543-6835). **Nearest Metro:** Capitol South on the Blue Line. **Hours for all three:** M-Sat, 11:00 am - 8:00 pm, closed Sun. **Credit Cards:** None. **Price:** INEXPENSIVE.

Some of my pals laughed when I told them I was going to include **Burrito Brothers**, the "California-Style Taqueria," thinking my book would be too chi-chi to include the Siblings of Burrito-dom. In fact, I dare any critic or fan of Mexican or Tex-Mex food to find a better Burrito in our fair city! It can't be done. **Burrito Brothers** is a small take-out or eat-standing-up place, but if you're in the mood for an authentic soft shell, flour tortilla burrito, this is the place.

The menu is small, offering **Burritos** and **Super Burritos** (40 percent larger). The choices include **Beans and Rice; Chicken; Roast Pork (Carnitas); Beef (Carne);** and **Spinach** (which I find okay but a little boring). You can get the same offerings in soft corn **Tacos**, which are also very good. The regular-size Burritos are big enough for most folks, and the Super Burritos are huge, come with cheese, and will readily satisfy two appetites.

The Burritos are filled with whole or refried pinto beans, Mexican rice, and chunks of tomato and salsa. The green chili hot sauce is made to order for those of us who like our food scorching - use it sparingly if you only want moderate heat.

CACTUS CANTINA

3300 Wisconsin Ave., NW, Washington, DC (202/686-7222). **Nearest Metro:** Tenleytown on the Red Line. **Hours:** M-Th, 11:00 am - 11:00 pm; F-Sat., 11:00 am - 11:45 pm; Sun., 11:00 am - 10:00 pm. **Credit Cards:** AE, CB, DC, DV, MC, V. **Price:** MODERATE.

Cactus Cantina has earned itself one of the best reputations for fine Mexican vittles this side of the border ... well, the Maryland/DC border, anyhow. It's almost always noisy and crowded, but the wait never seems too bad (especially with one of their great margaritas.

The **Salsa** is excellent: warm, spicy, with tomato chunks and cilantro. The **Nachos** are all right, but if you want to fill up on something before you chow down for real, try the **Quesadillas**, flour tortillas filled with beef or chicken and cheese.

The best options here are the **Fajitas**, prepared the standard way familiar to all Mexican food lovers but with a bit more care, less grease (they use peanut oil), and fresh vegetables and meat, grilled on mesquite. If you're in the mood to have your mouth sizzle with hot peppers, try the **Camarones Diablo**, or Devil's Shrimp. They're generously-spiced jumbo shrimp, broiled on a "sizzling" platter with Mexican butter, which tastes strangely like melted American butter! I like the **Enchiladas** here better than the **Tacos** or **Flautas**, which are decent enough but not their strong point. There is also the usual smattering of combination platters featuring enchiladas, tamales, and tacos, which are quite good.

Cactus Cantina has another strong point: the beer selection, seven of which are Mexican brews, including the dark beer lovers' choice, **Negra Modela**. When you're in the mood for a Tex-Mex meal that goes beyond the ordinary fare, try **Cactus Cantina**.

LA LOMITA

Two locations: 1330 Pennsylvania Ave., SE, Washington, DC (202/546-3109). **Nearest Metro:** Potomac Ave. on the Blue Line; and **La Lomita Dos**, 308 Pennsylvania Ave., SE, Washington, DC (202/544-0616). **Nearest Metro:** Capitol South on the Blue Line. **Hours:** M-F, 11:30 am - 3:00 pm, 5:00 pm -10:30 pm; Sat.-Sun., 5:00 pm - 10:30 pm. **Credit Cards:** AE, MC, V. **Price:** INEXPENSIVE.

La Lomita and *La Lomita Dos* are fun, homey Mexican joints, casual and festive. If you find yourself near the Hill or are visiting the museums on the Mall for the day, take a spin up Pennsylvania Ave. if your hungry for good Mexican food. The service is friendly and you can enjoy a smoke-free dinner upstairs.

The chips are standard fare, although the salsa (with a healthy dose of cilantro) is one of the better examples around. The **Quesadillas** and **Tamales** are good choices for your appetizers, if the chips don't suffice.

For entrées, I like the **Burritos** and **Enchiladas**; they're a good case of not screwing up the classics with a lot of fancy extras or too-heavy spicing. But the best offering here by far are the **Fajitas**, which come in several different varieties; I like the **Chicken Fajitas** best, but they're all good. If you're thirsty, the selection of **Mexican beers** is pretty good, and the **Margaritas** are hearty and hale.

There are fancier and, to be sure, better Mexican places around, but *La Lomita* ranks high on both the quality and value scales. Consider it next time you're up for a fun Mexican dinner.

MIXTEC

1792 Columbia Road, NW, Washington (202/332-1011). **Nearest Metro:** Dupont Circle on the Red Line. **Hours:** M-Th, 11:00 am - 10:30 pm; F-Sat., 11:00 am - 11:30 pm; Sun. 11:00 am - 10:30 pm. **Credit Cards:** MC, V. **Price:** INEXPENSIVE.

Located at the intersection of Columbia and 18th Street, the heart of Adams Morgan, **Mixtec** is a good, if not great, Mexican restaurant. There are enough deserving dishes on the menu to merit inclusion here, although some items are simply not up to par. Unlike most other Mexican restaurants, Mixtec does not provide you with complimentary chips and salsa.

I would start with what is perhaps Mixtec's best dish, the **Consomme Ranchero**, a delicious chicken broth with coriander and chopped onions. Stay away from the inconsistent **Rostizato**, their roasted chicken dish. The **Polle en Mole Mexicano** is a better choice (*Mole* - pronounced mo-lay) is a rich dark brown or reddish-brown chocoate sauce, prepared here with peppers, nuts, fruits, herbs and moderately hot spices); it is poured over chicken and served on a bed of rice.

Bistec a la Mexicana is also a good choice, which is sliced beef with tomatos, onions, and peppers cooked together with rice and beans. This too could use a more generous heaping of cayenne or chili powder, but it is tasty nevertheless. The **Vegetarian Burrito** (rice, beans, guacamole, and melted cheese) is one of the better non-meat dishes. The **Enchiladas** and **Tacos** here are just so-so.

If you're in the neighborhood, or are looking for a fairly decent Mole or Mexican steak dish, **Mixtec** is worth the visit. But you need to get the right dishes here. If you do, then **Mixtec** is a good value for your money.

MI RANCHO

8701 Ramsay Ave., Silver Spring, MD (301/588-4744). *Nearest Metro:* Silver Spring on the Red Line. *Hours:* M-Th, 11:00 am - 10:00 pm; F-Sat., 11:30 am - Midnight; Sun., 11:30 am - 10:00 pm. *Credit Cards:* AE, MC, V. *Price:* INEXPENSIVE.

When you step into *Mi Rancho*, you feel like you've walked into a cowboy's dream of a 1950's horse ranch. The decor is dark wood inside, not the fancy kind, but rather the homey kind. It's a down-to-earth Mexican joint, for my money as good a fajitas place as almost any around. Most District residents don't seem to know *Mi Rancho*, but they should - not because it's the last word on Mexican food, but because it's a good value. When they're crowded, though, service (while always friendly) cansometimes be a problem.

The chips and salsa are usually enough for me here, but their **Nachos** are also very good (real cheese used here), as are their **Tamales** - fresh, only a little greasy,and full of flavor.

As I said above, the best thing here are fajitas, which come in the usual variety: **Chicken Fajitas**, **Beef Fajitas**, **Shrimp Fajitas**, and the **Plato Grande**, for which you'd best bring a big appetite. The "Large Plate" consists of ribs, chicken, beef, shrimp, and guacamole, served with rice and beans. The chicken is juicy and moist, the beef tender, the shrimps big and fresh, and the spices are not overpowering. Grilled in its own juices, the fajitas dishes should definitely be part of your meal here. They're Silver Spring's answer to other fine Mexican eateries in Bethesda, DC, and Arlington.

You won't go wrong on the rest of the menu either, although here you're getting reliable but not great. The **enchiladas**, **tacos**, and **burritos** are good but not the best you'll ever have. The **Chimichanga**, however, is exemplary.

Stick to the fajitas and a few other dishes and you'll be fine. While *Mi Rancho's* service sometimes suffers, it's never at the expense of a fine meal.

RIO GRANDE CAFÉ

Three locations: 4919 Fairmont Ave., Bethesda, MD (301/656-2981). **Nearest Metro:** Bethesda on the Red Line; 4301 N. Fairfax Dr., Ballston, VA (703/528-3131). **Nearest Metro:** Ballston on the Orange Line; and 1827 Library St., Reston Town Center, Reston, VA (703/904-0703). **Nearest Metro:** N/A. **For all three - Hours:** M-Th, 11:00 am - 10:30 pm; F, 11:00 am - 11:30 pm; Sat., 11:30 am - 11:30 pm; Sun., 11:30 am - 10:30 pm. **Credit Cards:** AE, CB, DC, DV, MC, V. **Price:** MODERATE.

Rio Grande Café a popular and often crowded spot for good, solid Tex-Mex food, rose to instant prominence when former Commander-in-Chief George Bush, theoretically of Texas, made it one of his first dining out adventures (his taste for such food the result of Barbara forcing one too many broccoli spears on him).

The problem with *Rio Grande* is that it is very tough to just walk in off the street and get a table without a wait, sometimes 45 minutes and up, and not just on weekend nights. On Sunday afternoons, when you can get a table without too much trouble, be aware that the average age drops to about six. But *Rio Grande* offers a good, sometimes very good, variety of Tex-Mex dishes; the service is variable but friendly.

For appetizers, if the chips and excellent salsa are not enough, try the **Quesadillas**, which are flour tortillas filled with cheese or chicken, or the **Tamales**, beef-filled corn meal pastries.

The main goodies here are the **Fajitas**, which are some of the best fajitas in the area. They come in several ways: beef, chicken, shrimp, or in various combinations. **Tacos**, **burritos**, and **enchiladas** are all strong here; the **Chicken Enchiladas** in particular make a strong impression. I also like the **Camarones**, grilled shrimp in a buttery sauce. And the **Chiles Rellenos** is especially good; it's a semi-spicy dish made with poblano peppers stuffed with either beef or cheese.

Rio Grande is a loud, rollicking, good time, offering some of the finer area Tex-Mex food.

WELL DRESSED BURRITO

1220 19th St., NW, in the alley, Washington, DC (202/293-0515). **Nearest Metro:** Dupont Circle on the Red Line. **Hours:** M-F, 11:45 am - 2:30 pm. **Credit Cards:** None. **Price:** INEXPENSIVE.

This is the sole lunch-only restaurant I've included, but the quality and value of this small takeout place are so high that I figured it's no skin off my nose to include the good people at the **Well Dressed Burrito**. For those who are tired of always fulfilling their lunch-time Mexican cravings at the nearby and always excellent **Burrito Brothers**, here's a place with a down-home Tex-mex feel.

There are no appetizers here, but you've got a decent selection of entrées. Try the **Flauta**, deep-fried corn tortillas filled with your choice of five different fillings - spicy shredded beef, chicken in green and red tomato salsa, vegetables and mild chiles, several cheeses, or refried beans and cheese. The **Dos Tacos** and **Burrito** are also good, but I'd skip the rather flat **Chicken Empanada**, a deep-fried cornmeal turnover filled with chicken and cheese.

Two grilled dishes are particularly tasty: the **Chicken Fajitas**, marinated strips of chicken grilled with peppers and onions, refried beans, rice, guacamole and salsa, and the **Grilled Quesadilla**, a grilled flour tortilla with either chicken or beef, red chiles, and vegetables served with enchilada sauce, refried beans, rice, and salad. The *salsas* come in three varieties: mild, spicy, and hot, the latter almost worthy for those of us who enjoy our food best when our mouths are on fire and steam is venting from our ears! This hot and unique salsa (**Salsa Folks**) is made from five-chile salsa with red and green tomatoes and a touch of chocolate.

But the big winners here are the **El Gordo**, a large soft flour tortilla burrito with either chicken or beef and refried beans, topped with enchilada sauce, lettuce, tomato, rice and salsa; the **Well Dressed Chili**, beef chili in their five-chili sauce over rice, with cheese, scallions, cilantro, and sour cream; and the **Chimichanga**, a crispy fried flour tortilla with chicken or beef, topped with enchilada sauce. They're all three nicely seasoned and don't have that fast-food taste you might expect from a ... well, from a fast food place.

Too bad they're not open for dinner ...

CHICKEN AND STEAK A LA BRASA

Three locations: 320 D Street, NE (202/543-4633). **Nearest Metro:** Union Station on the Red Line; 5046 Lee Highway, Arlington, VA (703/237-8245). **Nearest Metro:** N/A; and 3410 Mt. Vernon St., Alexandria, VA (703/836-7150. **Nearest Metro:** N/A. **For all three - Hours:** M-Sat, 11:00 am -10:00 pm, closed Sun. **Credit Cards:** None. **Price:** INEXPENSIVE.

This small, simple restaurant, which does a fairly brisk lunch business from Senate staffers in Washington and beltway bandits in Arlington and Alexandria, is sort of the Peruvian equivalent of the Mexican fast-food joint Burrito Brothers, except you can sit down here. At **Chicken and Steak A La Brasa** (*a la brasa* loosely translates as "grilled"), they do Peruvian quickie chicken as good as anyone else in this class.

The **Rotisserie Charcoal Broiled Chicken** specials are the tops here. They're super-tender and moist, with the crispy skin trapping all those great spices. The chicken comes with a house salad and your choice of either fries, a ho-hum potato salad, or yuca (go with the yuca; you can get fries at McDonald's). The steaks are equally good, better than those offered by some of the other Peruvian chicken places that have expanded into beef. The pick of the lot is the **Marucha**, a top round of sirloin cooked in plenty of garlic and white wine sauce. It's delicioso.

Sandwiches may get the job done for you just as well; try the **Chorizo** (Spanish sausage) or **Chicken** sandwich. You can also combine some entrées and get the **Chicken and Steak** (which comes with a quarter broiled chicken and a 6 oz. filet mignon) or the **Mix Grilled**, a combo of rotisserie chicken, steak, pork, and chorizo. The latter really hits the spot and is the perfect choice when you can't choose between white meat or red.

Chicken and Steak A La Brasa gets my vote, along with the equally yummy El Pollo Rico, as best bets for fast-food Peruvian chicken and steak.

CRISP AND JUICY

Three locations. 4540 Lee Hwy., Arlington, VA (703/243-4222). **Nearest Metro:** N/A.; 3800 International Drive Ave. in Leisure World Plaza, Silver Spring (301/598-3333). **Nearest Metro:** N/A; and 1331G Rockville Pike in Sunshine Square shopping center. **For all three** - **Hours:** M-Sat 11:00 am - 10 pm, Sun. 11:00 am - 9 pm. **Credit Cards:** None. **Price:** INEXPENSIVE.

Crisp and Juicy is a Peruvian chicken place with an Argentinian twist, at least at the Arlington location.

The main event here is the **Roast Charbroiled Chicken (Pollo A Las Brasas)**, served as a quarter, half, or whole chicken. The chicken is indeed crisp and will squirt a fair amount of juice. The chefs have the Peruvian herbs and spice mixture down just about right. If you want to experiment with a few other items on the menu, order one of the charbroiled sandwiches, but if you're really hungry, try the aptly-named **Cannibal Platter**, featuring an excellent **Chorizo** (mild grilled sausage), **Carnita** (Argentinian steak), Peruvian-style sausage, and french fries.

For side dishes, I found the **Rice and Beans** fairly bland. The **Fried Yuca** (a thicker, heavier version of our french fries) is much better. But you'll want to stick to the basics here, at least at first, and go with one of their crisp and juicy *pollos*.

EL CHALAN

Two locations: 1924 I St., NW, Washington, DC (202/293-2765). **Nearest Metro:** Farragut West on the Blue Line; and 1654 Columbia Rd., NW, Washington, DC (202/797-9357). **Nearest Metro:** Dupont Circle on the Red Line. **For both** - **Hours :** Lunch, M-F, 11:30 am - 3:00 pm; Dinner daily, 5:30 pm - 11:00 pm. **Credit Cards:** AE, MC, V. **Price:** MODERATE.

El Chalan, a basement-level Peruvian restaurant, is proof-positive that not all good Peruvian places are fast-food joints. The menu is small, but the food is delicious, the service eager, and you're treated to more than just rotisserie chicken.

The *sopas* (soups) are a good place to start; I'd recommend either the **Crema de Pollo** (cream of chicken) or the **Chupe de Camarones** (Shrimp Bisque). The **Camarones A La Limeña**appetizer, shrimp tha tis just so-so, sautéed in a garlic butter sauce that's a bit too buttery. But do try two other appetizers: the **Ceviche De Pescado**, small chunks of seabass marinated in onions and lemon juice and sliced hot peppers, or the **Papa A La Huancaina**, boiled potatoes in a very tasty cream cheese-based peanut sauce.

If you like fish, you'll like the **Pescado A Lo Macho**, bass, clams, and shrimp baked in a white wine sauce. The **Aji De Gallina A La Arequipeña**, a shredded chicken dish cooked in a semi-spicy curry sauce. Other winners here include the traditional **Cabrito Norteño**, a succulent lamb stew served with rice and white beans, and the **Seco A La Huachana**, a beef stew also prepared with white beans and rice, but made with cilantro sauce. The beef dishes here pass the test of tenderness and taste. You can ask for a hot chili sauce that is pretty hot, but you'll find most dishes delicately spiced for us gringos.

This is a fine example of a growing Peruvian restaurant trend in the greater DC area. I hope they keep coming, and that their quality and value is as good as *El Chalan's*.

EL POLLO RICO

2915-2917 N. Washington Blvd., Arlington, VA (703/522-3220 or 522-3282). **Nearest Metro:** Clarendon on the Blue/Orange Line. **Hours:** 11:00 am - 10 pm daily. **Credit Cards:** None. **Price:** INEXPENSIVE.

El Pollo Rapido is more like it. Are Peruvians in a rush all the time, or do they love their food so much they can't get it quick enough? The meal is ready within seconds of ordering! Virtually all the great Peruvian joints around town seem to be fast food! No matter - **El Pollo Rico** is one of the best options in this category.

The menu is tiny, but there are only three things you want here anyway: **1/4 chicken**, **1/2 chicken**, or a **whole chicken.** In any size, the charcoal broiled chicken here is fantastic: moist and tender, with the skin crisp and perfectly spiced. The chicken comes with a very hot ground green chili pepper sauce, or a mild mayonnaise thing. If you don't like your food hot hot hot, but require a little kick, mix the two together and have at it.

Given how good the chicken is, it's a bit disappointing that the side dishes are not up to par. If you get anything else, skip the **Empanada** and **Tamale** and head straight for the **Tortilla Espanola de Papa**. If soft drinks are your bag, try the **Inka Cola**, a Peruvian drink that tastes a bit like cream soda. Two people can fill up quite nicely here for under $10!

THE CHICKEN PLACE

11201 Grandview Ave., Wheaton, MD (301/946-1212). **Nearest Metro:** Wheaton on the Red Line. **Hours:** M-Th, 11:30 am - 9:30 pm; F-Sat., 11:30 am - 11 pm; Sun., Noon - 10 pm. **Credit Cards:** AE, CB, DC, MC, V. **Price:** INEXPENSIVE.

Situated right across the street from the Wheaton Plaza, **The Chicken Place** now offers live music and dancing on weekends, in addition to some of the best Peruvian food around - all for a great low price. This place just keeps getting better and better.

The main event used to be their **Pollo a la Brasa**, rotisserie charcoal broiled chicken, served with white rice that tastes like it's been sprinkled with a dash of vinegar. It remains perhaps the best rotisserie chicken of its kind in the DC area. But now the menu has grown to include a full sampling of Peru's best grilled and fried delicacies.

For appetizers, the **Tamales** are super, filled with chicken, hard-boiled eggs, and olives. I haven't found the **Papa Rellena** elsewhere, which is too bad, because here it is out of this world: mashed potatoes wrapped in deep-fried potato flour, and filled with sautéed ground beef, onions, and a green "garnish" featuring diced jalapeño peppers. And while I'm not a huge fan of fish soup, the **Chilcano**, served with lemon and cilantro, may yet convert me.

For beef entrées, the various steak and beef stew dishes are superior, but the most interesting to me is the **Tacu Tacu con Bistec Apanado**, a tender grilled steak served atop pan-fried refried beans and rice cooked together in a delicious combination. For chicken - other than the rotisserie chicken already mentioned - try the **Aji de Gallina** (shredded chicken cooked in garlic, onions, parmesan cheese, milk and light spices, served over rice and potatoes) or the **Pollo Saltado** (grilled sliced chicken with onions, tomatoes, parsley, and spices, served with rice and french fries). Both are excellent.

The seafood choices should not be overlooked. Two of the best are the **Pescado a Lo "Chicken Place,"** fried trout with rice, cassava, and beans served in a fine onion sauce, and the **Picante de Mariscos**, a combo of sautéed shrimp, squid, octopus, and scallops, cooked in a light cream sauce and served with rice.

If you just order the broiled chicken, you're getting about the best sampling of Peruvian food around. But try some of the other dishes too for great quality and fantastic value.

ABI

3005 Columbia Pike, Arlington, VA (703/979-3579). *Nearest Metro:* N/A. *Hours:* 11:00 am - 10:00 pm, daily. *Credit Cards:* AE, MC, V. *Price:* INEXPENSIVE.

Restaurante Abi is easily the best Salvadoran value in town, and very possibly the best Central American value as well. The focus is clearly on the food; the decor is modest but the menu is extensive.

Start with the **Quesadilla Mexicana**, a fried tortilla topped with either cheese, beef, or chicken, with guacamole and sour cream; the **Pupusas**, fried corn meal filled with pork and cheese (or beans); or the **Tamal De Pollo**, corn meal wrapped in a banana leaf stuffed with chicken and vegetables.

For your entrée, you've got a huge selection. If you like seafood, you'll like the **Camarones al Ajillo**, jumbo shrimp sautéed in white wine and garlic butter and served over rice. For chicken, I prefer the **Pollo Entomatado**, sautéed chunks of chicken in a mildly spicy tomato sauce, served with rice and beans. The long suit here, though, are the *carne* (beef) platters, including their **Fajitas**. Two especially good steaks are the **Carne Picada**, strips of steak sautéed with onions, tomatoes, and green peppers, served with rice and beans; and the **Lomo Saltado**, steak slices sautéed with olive oil, onions, potatoes, and tomatoes.

The Mexican dishes are also quite good; their burritos and chimichangas are as good as any Mexican restaurant in these here parts. There are also a number of combination dishes you may want to consider, mostly featuring enchiladas, tacos, tamales, and pupusas.

Desserts here are more unusual than the standard selection in most ethnic restaurants. I especially like the **Nuegados**, a delicious yuca mix with ground and fried cheese, topped with caramel.

For the money, it's hard to find a better deal than *Abi.*

ATLACATL

Two locations: 2716 N. Washington Blvd., Arlington, VA (703/524-9032); and 2602 Columbia Pike, Arlington, VA (703/920-3680). **Nearest Metro:** . **Hours:** M-Th, 11:00 am - 10:30 pm; F-Sat., 11:00 am - 12:30 am; Sun., 11:00 am - 11:00 pm. **Price:** MODERATE.

Atlacatl is not a fancy place, but consistently delivers solid Salvadoran and Mexican food (although the best choices here are Salvadoran). If you're looking for authentic Central American fare, this is one place you ought to visit.

Start off with one of the sopas (soups), or perhaps the **Guacamole Dip** with pieces of fried flour tortilla, the **Pupusas** (thick tortillas filled with either white cheese, pork, beans, or herbs), or a basket of **Yuca** - also known as casaba or manioc root. They look like fat french fries, and Atlacatl has the best in town. This is really a side dish; while you can order a more elaborate Yuca appetizer, I never seem to be able to get past the simple Yuca "fries."

The Mexican portion of the menu is all right but doesn't do too much for me; I find the **El Burro Grande** too salty and the melted cheese on the watery side. But for some reason the Salvadoran entrées don't seem to suffer the same fate. The combination dishes throw together pupusas, enchiladas, tacos, yuca and tamales. On the specialties (*Especialidades*) menu, I'd recommend either the **Especial Atlacatl I** or **II**: the first is pork filet topped with sausage and cheese, served with refried beans, salad, and rice; the second is sautéed steak done the same way, with the same accompaniments. If you want a more hearty broiled steak, try the **Carne Asada A La Salvadorena**, which come with a tortilla smothered in cheese.

Other winners here are the **Camarones Al Ajillo**, sautéed shrimp cooked in a garlic butter sauce, served with Spanish rice and salad, and the **Pollo Encebollado** (sautéed chicken with Salvadoran sauce, topped with sautéed onions and fried potatoes).

Atlacatl is one of the very best Salvadoran eateries in the area, and should definitely be on your list of Central American places to try.

MIDDLE EASTERN & SOUTH ASIAN

BAMIYAN II

"Olde Town Bamiyan," aka Bamiyan II, 300 King Street, Old Town (703/548-9006). **Nearest Metro:** King Street on the Blue Line. **Hours: Nearest Metro:** N/A. **Price:** MODERATE.

Don't confuse **Bamiyan II** in Old Town, Alexandria, with the Georgetown Bamiyan; they are different restaurants with different owners and menus. The decor in **Bamiyan II** is nice but modest, with photos from the old country, a big plaster Buddha and paintings of Afghan horsemen raising a lot of dust — possibly intended to induce great thirst. The menu still has an inside page asking for freedom from occupation by the Soviet Union (if memory serves, I think that was once a big country with a heck of a lot of time zones, whose soldiers were notorious for leaving small tips in the restaurants of the various countries they occupied). But enough tomfoolery — for my cash, **Bamiyan II** is the best Afghan restaurant in the area.

The menu is small here, but almost every dish is a winner. Start with **Bulaunee**, a crispy turnover appetizer stuffed with scallions, herbs and ground beef. Yogurt is served on the side, and makes a good dipping sauce. This could be a pretty greasy dish, but not here: it's light and perfectly seasoned. **Aushak**, which can also be had as a main dish, is another good choice for starters; it's a dumpling filled with scallions and topped with yogurt and meat sauce, with a mint garnish. It's not as exciting as the bulaunee, but it's respectable nonetheless.

The **Kebab-e-Murgh** is unquestionably one of the best chicken dishes I've ever had in this or any other town. The chicken is marinated in herbs and spices and served on a skewer with brown rice. The main flavorings that makes this dish sing are yogurt, garlic, and red and black pepper. The **Sabsi Chalow** is a great lamb dish, served in chunks in an onion and garlic flavored spinach sauce on a bed of white rice. For a side dish, try the **Kadu**, which is sautéed pumpkin topped with yogurt and a very tasty meat sauce. If your tastes run to veggies, the eggplant dishes (**Buraunee**) are also well worth the price.

Portions are large here — the entrées come with a salad — so bring your appetite!

KABUL CARAVAN

1725 Wilson Blvd., Arlington, VA (703/522-8394). *Nearest Metro:* Court House on the Orange Line. *Hours:* M-F, 11:30 am - 2:30 pm, 5:30 pm - 11:00 pm; Sat.-Sun, 5:30 pm - 11:00 pm. *Credit Cards:* AE, MC, V. *Price:* MODERATE.

Since 1979 - the year that many Afghanis came to the West in search of safe haven from Soviet guns - this particular caravan has been cooking up traditional Afghan cuisine, in a colorful setting filled with treasures from the home country. Bright costumes, fine jewelry, aging muskets, and tarnished swords adorn the walls and set the right mood for a first-rate meal.

Start with the expertly-prepared **Aushak**, those scallion-filled dumplings made with yogurt and meat sauce and topped with crushed mint leaves. If you want something with a little bite, order the **Bolany Kachlo**, a fried turnover filled with potatoes and onions, and accompanied with a hot green sauce. Or you may want to try one of their soups: go with the **Aush**, a noodle and vegetable soup made with yogurt, mint, spices, and ground beef.

There are some fine vegetarian specials, particularly the **Banjan Palow**, an eggplant dish with onions, tomatoes, and spices, topped with yogurt and served over brown rice. I also like the **Zamarud Chalow**, thick pieces of lamb cooked in spinach and spices (particularly cardamom), served over rice. Other winners here are the kabab, especially the **Kabab Shamy** (spiced ground beef, chickpeas, and vegetables broiled on a skewer) and the **Kabab Mergh** (marinated boneless chicken breast pieces, cooked with garlic and assorted spices). My favorite dish is still **Manto**, ground beef with onions, served with dumplings filled with yogurt, and all topped off with coriander.

For side dishes, don't miss the **Borane Kadu**, sautéed pumpkin topped with yogurt and meat sauce. The desserts are good here, but very sweet; the **Gosh-E-Fell**, also known as "Elephant's Ear," is a thin pastry served with powdered sugar.

Like many Afghan restaurants, *Kabul Caravan* could offer a larger selection. But all in all, one of the better Afghan places around!

KABUL WEST

4871 Cordell Avenue, Bethesda (301/986-8566). *Nearest Metro:* Bethesda on the Red Line. *Hours:* M-Th, 11:30 am - 2:00 pm, 5:00 pm - 10:00 pm; F, 11:30 am - 2:00 pm, 5:00 pm - 11:00 pm; Sat., 5:00 pm - 11:00 pm; Sun., 5:00 pm - 10:00 pm. *Credit Cards:* MC, V. *Price:* MODERATE-TO-EXPENSIVE.

Some reviewers are starting to give *Kabul West* a hard time, and I can see their point. The price has gone up more than is warranted with no noticeable change in the quality of the food or the ambiance, which is nice (hanging rugs and typical Afghan art on the walls), but not that incredible. Overall the food is still good here, and some dishes remain very good, but competition is getting stiffer.

The **Aushak** (scallion-filled dumplings topped with yogurt and meat sauce) is adequate, but much better is the **Bulanee** (spelled *Bulaunee* at some other restaurants), fried turnovers stuffed with spiced scallions and herbs. On the greasy side in some restaurants, here the Bulanee is delicate, very tasty, and not greasy. The **Aush**, a delicious soup, made with yogurt (what else? yogurt is the staple seasoning in Afghan cooking), vegetables, and noodles, topped with a meat sauce, is a clear winner.

Lamb and chicken dishes are the best here, while the vegetarian selection is good but mixed. If you like lamb, try either the **Kabab-e-Gousfand**, strips of lamb in an impressive meat sauce; the **Sabsi Chalow**, chunks of lamb in a great onion-garlic spinach sauce; or the **Quabili Palow**, lamb chunks mixed in with saffron rice, carrots, and raisins. Each dish is either accompanied by rice or served over rice. The **Chalow Badenjan**, a stew of eggplant and onions, was not terribly exciting.

All in all, there are cheaper Afghan restaurants that offer better value. But *Kabul West* still has some quality Afghan cuisine to offer, served in a pleasant setting.

ADITI

3299 M St., NW, Washington, DC (202/625-6825). *Nearest Metro:* N/A. *Hours:* M, 5:30 pm - 10:00 pm; T-Th., 11:30 am - 2:30 pm, 5:30 pm - 10:00 pm; F-Sat., 11:30 am - 2:30 pm, 5:30 pm - 10:30 pm. *Credit Cards:* AE, CB, DC, DV, MC, V. *Price:* MODERATE.

Located in historic Georgetown, just a few blocks from the Key Bridge, *Aditi* offers reasonably-priced Indian food in an elegant setting. The service is friendly and the menu, while not extensive, has a nice variety of India's different culinary traditions, including some great vegetarian curry dishes.

For appetizers, they do a fine job on the **Bhajia** (crushed vegetables dipped in flour paste and deep-fried) the Vegetable **Samosa** (a fried turnover filled with spicy potatoes and green peas), and the **Paneer Pakora** (cheese slices dipped in chickpea paste and deep-fried).

From the tandoori world, I'd go for the **Chicken Tikka**, boneless chicken pieces cooked in traditional spices and herbs, and cooked on skewers in a clay oven *(tandoor* refers to cooking in a clay oven). The **Murgh Sheesh Kabab**, chicken breast marinated in yogurt and spices and cooked on skewers with tomatoes, onions, and bell peppers, is another fine choice here. If you like your food hot, try the **Lamb Vindaloo**, boneless lamb chunks and potatoes cooked in a spicy sauce; I also like the less spicy **Rogan Josh**, lamb cubes cooked in a tomato sauce with various Indian spices.

From the vegetarian list, I'd recommend the **Saag Paneer**, spinach and cheese cooked in a curry sauce; the **Dal**, which are black lentils seasoned with spices and herbs; and the **Bengan Bharta**, tandoori-style eggplant, cooked with tomatoes, onions, and spices. The breads do not disappoint, and the side dishes are better than the usual deal; in addition to the **Raita** (yogurt blended with chopped cucumbers and roasted cumin seeds), I'd strongly recommend the **Kachumber**, not found elsewhere in this area to my knowledge: diced cucumbers, tomatoes, bell peppers, lettuce, and onions, topped with *Chat Masala* (spicy vegetables mixed with various spices) and yogurt.

If you prefer vegetarian, you might want to consider this place above others, because this is one of their specialties. But wherever your tastes run, check out *Aditi* for an exemplary Indian dining experience.

BOMBAY BISTRO

98 W. Montgomery Ave., Rockville, MD (301/762-8798). *Nearest Metro:* N/A. *Hours:* Lunch, M-F, 11 am - 2:30 pm; Sat-Sun, Noon - 3 pm; Dinner, Sun-Th, 5 pm - 9:30 pm; F-Sat., 5 pm - 10 pm. *Credit Cards:* MC, V. *Price:* INEXPENSIVE-TO-MODERATE.

Bombay Bistro is a great find. Not far from downtown Rockville, it's a bit of a drive up Rockville Pike for Districtites, but well worth it. Nice ambiance, friendly service - and, always a good sign, it gets the 'expat' seal of approval (most of the regulars are of South Asian origin).

For appetizers, try the **Papri Chat**, flour crisps with diced potatoes, served in a delicious yogurt and sweet and sour sauce; the **Samosa**, a crisp pastry stuffed with potatoes and peas; or the **Bhel Puri**, a combo of rice puffs and crisp noodles, with spring onions cut into the mix.

The main selections are filled with winners! If you're a Tandoori fan, try the **Chicken Malai Kabab**, grilled chicken breasts marinated in yogurt, cilantro, and hot peppers. If curry's your thing, go for the **Lamb Nilgiri Khorma** (direct from South India, the Nilgiri Khorma is chunks of lamb smothered in a spicy green masala sauce) or the **Chicken Madras**, less spicy and very tender. In the vegetarian corner, I'd go with either the **Vegetable Jhalfrezi**, a mix of nicely-flavored sautéed veggies, or the **Peshawari Chole**, chickpeas and potatoes cooked in a great sauce from the old northwestern corner of the Raj.

You ought to try one of the **Dosa's**, if you haven't already. Practically a staple of South Indian cuisine, the dosa's, which are sort of like long flat pancakes or crepes, are made either with lentils and rice; spiced potatoes and onion masala; semolina and rice; and other combinations.

The **Raita**, an "accompaniment" made from homemade yogurt, grated cucumbers, and roasted cumin seeds, is particularly good here, as is the **Dal Makhani**, black lentils and tomatoes simmered in ginger. You have five breads to choose from, all fresh and delicious. For dessert, the **Kulfi** (not on the menu) is excellent (sort of like a half-frozen sweet cream); and, while not to everyone's taste, you might want to try the **Shreekhand**, both because the name is so evocative and for the sake of trying something most other local Indian restaurants don't offer. Shreekhand is ice cream-like, made with pistachio, yogurt, and saffron.

Bombay Bistro is justly deserving of all the awards it's won. And what you spend on gas getting here will be more than made up for when you get the bill.

BOMBAY CLUB

815 Connecticut Ave., NW, Washington (202/659-3727). **Nearest Metro:** Farragut North on Red Line or Farragut West on Blue Line. **Hours: . Credit Cards:** M-Th, 11:30 am - 2:30 pm, 6:00 pm - 10:30 pm; F, 11:30 am - 2:30 pm, 6:00 pm - 11:00 pm; Sat., 6:00 pm - 11:00 pm; Sun., 11:30 am - 2:30 pm (brunch), 5:30 pm - 9:00 pm. **Price:** EXPENSIVE.

The British raj is alive and well at the **Bombay Club**, just a few blocks from the White House. The atmosphere here is exactly what the name says: a clubby, plush decor — an exclusive and elegant meeting house open to all who care to fork over at least $30-$40 or more per person for a full meal with drinks. The service is attentive and authentic; most of the Indian waiters speak the King's English with an Etonian accent. Polo anyone, what?

Every now and then, though, the quality is inconsistent. It's never bad, but sometimes lacks any firepower or even flavor, and for that kind of dough, you expect more. Still, when they're in top form, it's a great meal.

Two appetizers I especially like are the **Seekh Kebab**, grilled and skewered minced lamb rolls spiced with coriander, and **Sev Puri**, a number of crispy *puris* (deep-fried puffy bread) topped with potatoes, mangoes, onions, an Indian spice called *sev*, mint, dates, and tamarind sauce. Both are wonderful creations expertly prepared here.

The tandoor specialty to get here is the **Tandoori Chicken**, a nice-sized barbecued spring chicken marinated overnight in yogurt, ginger, and garlic. The chicken melts in your mouth, not in your stomach. Advertised as "not for the faint hearted," the **Green Chili Chicken** is one of those on-again, off-again dishes, but when they're on, watch out! Cooked over a slow fire, the spices are coriander, green chiles and green herbs. The **Lamb Roganjosh**, a Moghul specialty, is another great choice, lamb chunks cooked with saffron, yogurt, and spices, served with **Roti** (whole wheat flour) bread.

Two first-rate vegetarian side dishes dishes are **Baingan Bharta**, grilled eggplant cooked with onion, tomato, and herbs, and the **Aloo Palak**, spinach and potatoes flavored with a *masala* of herbs. And don't forget the last course, or at least one killer dessert in particular: **Kulfi with Fresh Berries**, an Indian ice cream (really heavy frozen cream) served with - get this - *poached* berries and topped with crème-de cassis.

Most of the time, **Bombay Club** serves excellent food in a refined, courtly atmosphere. If you're looking for that special occasion kind of place, this could well be it.

BOMBAY PALACE

2020 K St., NW, Washington, DC (202/331-4200). **Nearest Metro:** Farragut North on Red Line or Farragut West on Blue Line. **Hours:** Lunch daily, Noon - 2:30 pm; M-Th, 5:30 pm - 10:30 pm; F-Sat., 5:30 pm - 11:00 pm; Sun., 5:30 pm - 10:00 pm. **Credit Cards:** AE, CB, DC, MC, V. **Price:** MODERATE.

Why is it that so many fine Indian restaurants seem to trace their lineage to Bombay, India's grand old city on the Arabian Sea? The short answer is they don't! The food here, as in most Indian restaurants in this country, is **Punjabi** in origin (Punjab is a state in northwest India), except for the *vindaloo* specialties, which hail from the former Portuguese colony of Goa off India's southwestern coast. So why isn't this the *Punjab Palace*? Who knows? The food is so good at **Bombay Palace**, you won't be troubling yourself with such thoughts.

Now in their new digs a block away and across the street from their old address, the Palace is brighter and more elegant than ever. And the food remains first-rate. For appetizers, try the **Chicken Pakora** (chicken fritters made out of chick pea flour and served in a nice sharp sauce); **Bhel Puri**, a mixture of puffed rice crisps, lentil vermicelli, and chutney; or the old standby **Samosa**, a flaky turnover stuffed with potatoes and peas, spiced with coriander, cumin, and red chilis.

In the entrée department, the tandoori chicken dishes are excellent, but for something special, go for the **Lamb Chops Kandahari**, actually an Afghani dish that has been "tandoori-ized," consisting of grilled lamb chops marinated with ginger and a *masala* of Indian spices, like cardamom, cumin, cloves, etc. The **Prawns Masala** are terrific, jumbo prawns sautéed in ginger, garlic, onions, and tomatoes. Consider also the *murgh* (chicken) specialties, especially the **Chicken Keema** (sliced chicken cooked in ginger, garlic, cilantro, and diced tomato). If you like it hot, try one of the **Vindaloos**, either lamb or seafood; the active ingredient is a lot of red curry sauce. There's a big assortment of vegetarian dishes too; the **Channa Masala**, garbanzo beans cooked in onions, tomatoes, Indian spices and tamarind (a sweet citrus) sauce. The various breads, side dishes, and rice dishes are without peer.

Measured in terms of quality or value, **Bombay Palace** is the best Indian restaurant in town.

HAANDI

Two locations: 4904 Fairmont Ave., Bethesda, MD (301/718-0121). **Nearest Metro:** Bethesda on the Red Line; and 1222 W. Broad St., Falls Church, VA (703/533-3501). **Nearest Metro:** West Falls Church on the Blue/Orange Line. **Hours for both:** Sun.-F, 11:30 am - 2:30 pm, 5:00 pm - 10:00 pm; Sat., 5:00 - 10:00 pm; closed Mon. **Credit Cards:** AE, MC, V. **Price:** MODERATE.

Haandi - formerly Masala in the Bethesda location - is without a doubt one of the very best gourmet Indian restaurants in the area, and it's reasonably priced to boot. The decor is quite nice, although running a tad too much on the pink-pastel side for me.

The appetizers, which come with *Haandi's* own green coriander chutney (putting most other chutneys to shame), are excellent. The appetizers are all so good that I'd recommend the **Assorted Appetizer Platter**; you get **Samosas** (deep-fried turnovers filled with spicy potatoes and peas), **Sabzi Pakora** (fritters cooked in chick pea batter stuffed with eggplant, cauliflower, onions, and potatoes), **Murg Tikka** (chicken breast pieces marinated in yogurt, herbs, and spices), and **Botti Kebab** (grilled lamb pieces similarly marinated to the Murg Tikka). They're easily as good as any other comparable dishes in town.

For entrées, I'm particularly fond of the **Murg Reshmi Tandoori**, a mild dish of chicken pieces marinated in green herbs and yogurt, cooked tandoori style over a charcoal clay oven, and served with long-grain basmati rice sprinkled with saffron and wild black cardamom. The **Channa Masala** and the **Daal Masala** are superb vegetarian dishes, the former a chick pea dish cooked with potatoes in a semi-spicy sauce, the latter a mixture of different kinds of lentils cooked in mild spices.

The **Rogan Josh** is perhaps the best of its kind in the metropolitan area, tender chunks of lamb cooked in a creamy yogurt curry sauce, lightly flavored with basil. The **Dhanwal Korma**, chicken pieces cooked over a slow fire with coriander, green chilies, green herbs, and yogurt. And if you want something really hot, go for the **Vindalu**, chunks of lamb and potatoes in a hot, spicy red curry sauce.

At twice the price, Haandi would still be quite a deal. As it is, this is Indian dining at its finest, all for a modest price tag.

IMPERIAL INDIA CLUB

4931 Cordell Avenue, Bethesda, MD (301/656-3373). *Nearest Metro:* Bethesda on the Red Line. *Hours:* Sun.-F, 11:30 am - 2:30 pm; 5:30 pm - 10:00 pm, daily. *Credit Cards:* AE, DC, DV, MC, V. *Price:* MODERATE.

Small but elegant, the *Imperial India Club* is yet another Indian restaurant going for that clubby feel. The atmosphere is warm and cozy, the service is very good, and the food is usually on target.

The appetizers here are consistently good. The **Spinach Pakora** is the best pick, a deep-fried fritter of spinach and chick peas served with mint sauce. It's as grease-free as you can make a fritter, which ain't easy. The **Aloo Bonda**, a thin shell of chick pea batter stuffed with potatoes, cashews and mustard seeds, and the **Masala Puri**, a lentil and flour dish with tomatoes, potatoes, cashew nuts, and onions in a sweet and sour sauce, are both terrific.

There are several very good vegetarian specialties, served with basmati rice. **Dal** (lentils) is served with a number of dishes here, and, if one wore a hat, one would take it off in homage and deep respect to the chef: chances are good you haven't had lentils like these before! If you want to get a good flavor of the vegetarian dishes, try the **Raj Thali**, an assortment dish where you get to try the **Palak Paneer** (a delicious Punjabi spinach dish that is not too hot but still has a nice kick); the **Baingan Bharata** (grilled eggplant cooked with onions, tomatoes, and Indian herbs); and the **Mili Jhuli Tarkari** (beans, carrots, potatoes, cauliflower, bell peppers and green peas cooked in a mild curry sauce).

If you want an assortment of meat dishes, order the **Imperial Thali**. You get **Shrimp Masala** (which is excellent), **Chicken Makhani** (sauce was a bit heavy and uninspiring), the **Chicken Tikka** (another Punjabi specialty, featuring chicken simmered in tomato and honey sauce topped with coriander), and **Josh**, cubes of lamb cooked with saffron, yogurt, and various spices (all fairly mild). All the dishes in these samplers are, of course, on the menu and can be ordered individually.

The sauces here are memorable; they are not heavy at all and the spicing is just right. The breads are all good choices. Just pick the one that appeals to you and you won't go wrong. While not inexpensive, the *Imperial India Club* offers fine dining and a more than decent value.

POLO INDIA CLUB

1736 Connecticut Ave., NW Washington (202/483-8705). *Nearest Metro:* Dupont Circle on the Red Line. *Hours:* M-Th, 11:30 am - 2:30 pm, 5:30 pm - 10:30 pm; F-Sat., 11:30 am - 2:30 pm, 5:30 pm - 11:00 pm; Sun., 5:30 pm - 10:30 pm. *Credit Cards:* AE, DC, DV, MC, V. *Price:* MODERATE.

New on Washington's Indian dining scene, the *Polo India Club* is a welcome addition to an already fine stable - if I can use that word in a culinary context - of gracious and courtly South Asian restaurants. The decor is almost fern bar-esque, although there are some polo mallets and helmets perched on one of the walls. My guess is that they are trying to emulate, on a smaller scale, the kind of colonial-era cachet that Bombay Club uniquely has in this town.

The appetizers are very good; you might want to try the **Appetizer Platter** for a sampling of each taste offered. The **Samosa** (triangle pastry stuffed with spiced potatoes and peas), **Bhajiya** (cauliflower, onion, potato, and spinach fritters cooked in chick pea batter), **Paneer Pakora** (cubed cottage cheese dipped in chick pea batter and deep-fried), and **Leko** (crisply-fried, marinated, lightly spiced chicken pieces dipped in chick pea batter) are light and not at all greasy. The portions are not generous, however, so get two if you're hungry.

The entrées are also sparse, but with only a few exceptions, are mostly good. If you like Tandoori, which along with Biryani dishes are the house specialties, try the **Malai Chicken Tikka**, a mildly-flavored Tandoori-style chicken breast marinated in fresh herbs and yogurt, barbecued in a clay oven, and served with nicely-spiced grilled onions on the side. The chicken was moist and tender, but not a hint of the reddish coloring that characterizes Tandoori food. The **Lamb Saag**, chunks of lamb cooked in spinach and herbs, is excellent, as is the **Polo Jaipuri Chicken**, boneless chicken pieces marinated with "special Himalayan herbs" cooked in a charcoal clay oven and soaked in the chef's creamy, yellow Jaipuri sauce, that was done just right.

But stay away from the **Chicken** or **Lamb Vindaloo**, unless you prefer your vindaloo on the bland and relatively unspicy side. There is some heat, but not nearly enough, and the spicing is merely adequate. Again, the portions are small. The breads are good, but nothing out of the ordinary.

For dessert, try the **Khulfi Saffron**, which is described as ice cream but is really frozen heavy cream with saffron sauce and topped with raspberry and strawberry sauce. The coffee is fine, but if you want a real Indian taste, order the **Punjabi Tea**, which is seasoned with cloves, cinnamon and cardamom. The service is attentive without being overbearing or hovering.

BACCHUS

Two locations: 1827 Jefferson Pl., NW, Washington, DC (202/785-0734). **Nearest Metro:** Dupont Circle on the Red Line; and 7945 Norfolk Ave., Bethesda, MD (301/657-1722). **Nearest Metro:** Bethesda on the Red Line. **Hours:** M-F, Noon - 2:00 pm, 6:00 - 10:00 pm, (F, 6:00 pm - 10:30 pm); Sat., 6:00 pm - 10:30 pm; Bacchus-Bethesda open Sun., 6:00 pm - 10:00 pm. **Credit Cards:** AE, MC, V. **Price:** MODERATE.

Bacchus remains among the best Middle Eastern establishments in the Washington area. You can now enjoy this restaurant in its Bethesda location too. The downtown **Bacchus** is much smaller and cozier, while the Bethesda branch is less formal and bigger.

The odd thing about the menu, which is extensive, is that you've got five pages of appetizers and only two of entrées, which tells you to load up on the first course and tread lightly on the second. Whether you order nothing but appetizers or go the usual route, you won't be disappointed.

My favorite entrées include **Shawarma**, thinly-sliced marinated lamb, tomatoes and onions, served with a delicious yogurt-based sauce; **Yalani Bethenjan**, eggplant stuffed with rice, onions, pomegranate sauce and spices, cooked in olive oil; **Hommos Bel Foul**, your basic hummos (chick pea puree with sesame paste) dressed up with garlic, lemon juice, and topped with fava beans and olive oil; and **I Jeh**, a soft and tasty dish resembling a baked vegetable quiche, with chopped zucchini, parsley, onions, and spices. But these appetizers really just scratch the surface; I've tried most of the appetizers here and they are all superb.

The entrée selection, as noted above, is a bit sparse, but the quality is of the highest. Among the best are the **Fatte Del Lahm**, tender chunks of lamb, cooked in "sizzling butter," and served atop a winning combination of deep-fried Lebanese bread, yogurt, and garlic; **Sedr Djaj Mechwi**, chicken breast spiced mildly and marinated in garlic; and **Shish Taouk**, grilled chicken cubes marinated in olive oil, lemon, garlic, and spices, served on rice with almonds and pine nuts. There are several Lebanese wines, both red and white, but they're fairly boring.

If you like Middle Eastern food, you'll love **Bacchus**.

LEBANESE TAVERNA

Two locations: 2641 Connecticut Ave., NW (202/265-8681). *Nearest Metro:* Woodley Park-Zoo on the Red Line. *Hours:* M-Th, 11:30 am - 3:00 pm; F, 11:30 am - 3:00 pm, 5:00 - 11:00 pm; Sat. 11:00 am - 11:00 pm; Sun., 5:00 - 10:00 pm; and 5900 Washington Blvd., Arlington, VA (703/241-8681). *Nearest Metro:* N/A. *Hours:* Same as above, except it's closed Sundays and holidays. *Price:* MODERATE.

Lebanese Taverna has quickly become one of the best Middle Eastern restaurants in the Washington area. The atmosphere is Middle Eastern enough to put you in the mood to try something different, but not overdone like some Middle East restaurants, where you feel like you're trapped inside Jeannie's bottle.

If you like pine nuts, you'll like *Lebanese Taverna*; they find their way into many dishes. There's a good selection of vegetarian appetizers, including a mean **Baba Ghannouge** (baked eggplant pureed with sesame paste, lemon juice and garlic, topped with olive oil) and a very interesting dish you ought to try called **Loubieh Bel Zeit**, a mixture of string beans, tomatoes, garlic and various spices cooked in olive oil. It's served at room temperature. The **Falafel**, while serviceable, needs a little work. One of my favorite dishes here is the **Manakish D'Sbanigh**, a pizza-like pie topped with spinach, onion and pine nuts, which cannot be recommended strongly enough; for meat-lovers, another pizza rip-off dish that tastes better than it looks is the **Lahem Bel Ajin**, baked ground beef cooked with spices, parsley, herbs, and pine nuts.

For entrées, both the **Shish Taouk** and the **Farouj** are good choices if you're in the mood for chicken; the former is grilled cubes of chicken breast on a skewer of tomatoes, onions, and green peppers, the latter is a half-chicken cooked on a rotisserie and wrapped in a Middle Eastern bread similar to a pita, only lighter. A more exciting chicken dish, however, is the **Fatteh Bel Djaj**, perfectly-seasoned chicken pieces served on toasted pita and chick peas, drowned in yogurt and sautéed butter. The **Shawarma** is one of their best dishes. It's thinly-sliced marinated beef and lamb, tomatoes and onions, roasted on a rotisserie, like the Farouj. The **Lamb Shish Kabob** is a reliable standard, but if you want to be a bit more adventurous, try the calorie-filled **Sharhat Ghanam** (thinly-sliced grilled lamb served in lemon garlic and butter sauce).

There are only a few good Middle Eastern restaurants around here, and one of them is *Lebanese Taverna*.

PERSEPOLIS

7130 Wisconsin Ave., Bethesda, MD (301/656-9339). **Nearest Metro:** Bethesda on the Red Line. **Hours:** Noon - 11:00 pm, daily. **Credit Cards:** AE, CB, DC, MC, V. **Price:** MODERATE.

Persepolis is one of those on-again, off-again places. More often than not I've been happy with the food here, but every so often something seems to go amiss in the kitchen, so consider this my qualifier. Still, when it's on, the kebabs and some of the other delicacies are impressive.

For appetizers, go with the **Kashk-o Bademjan**, sautéed eggplant, cooked in onions, herbs, and spices and mixed with sour cream; and the **Dolmeh Barg-e Moe**, stuffed grape leaves filled with sautéed ground sirloin, scallions, rice, herbs, and spices, cooked in a sweet-and-sour sauce (less heavy than the kind you may be used to in Chinese restaurants).

The kabob entrées are the best things here, although the **Fessanjan**, a *khoresh*-style dish (basically a stew) made with braised chicken pieces, pomegranate sauce, sugar, and ground walnuts, is quite good. The two best kebabs are the **Chelo Kabob-o Chenjeh**, chunks of strip steak marinated in onions andPersian seasonings; and the **Jujeh Kabob**, boneless chicken breast marinated in saffron and various spices. The **Kabob-e Barreh**, a lamb-loin kabob, is sometimes tender and right on the money, and other times tough and chewy.

Desserts are your standard, too-sweet fare, but if you've got a sweet tooth, try the **Zulbia-Bamieh**, a saffron-flavored pastry. There are other interesting Persian restaurants in the area, but *Persepolis*is one of the better examples around.

KAZAN

6813 Redmond Dr., McLean, VA (703/734-1960). **Nearest Metro:** N/A. **Hours:** Lunch, M-F, 11:00 am - 2:00 pm; Dinner, M-Sat., 5:30 pm - 11:00 pm; closed Sun. **Credit Cards:** AE, MC, V. **Price:** HIGH MODERATE.

Kazan has a richly deserved reputation for serving fine food in an Old World Turkish setting. The service is efficient and friendly, the menu extensive, and the food hard to beat. The specials are usually very good here, so you may want to see what's being offered the night you're here.

You've got an extensive list of appetizers to choose from, but two of my favorites are the **Borek Karisik**, small fried pastries, half stuffed with cheese, half with spinach; and the **Imam Bayildi**, eggplant stuffed with green peppers, onions, and tomatoes, cooked in olive oil and served cold.

On Wednesday, Friday, and Saturday, try the **Döner Kebab**, the best in the area. As prepared at **Kazan**, this Turkish specialty is thinly sliced marinated lamb and veal, served either with rice alone or over spicy yogurt sauce and sautéed tomatoes and melted butter. Not too rich!!! Other favorites include **Halep Kebab**, grilled *kofte* (spicy chopped lamb) served over sautéed eggplant and tomatoes, green peppers, and onions, with grilled pita bread slices; the **Turkish Manti**, small pasta shells stuffed with lamb, covered in a creamy and gently spiced yogurt and garlic sauce; and the delicious **Pılıç Yogurtlu Kebab**, chunks of chicken sautéed in tomato butter, served over toasted pita chunks and topped with yogurt sauce.

Desserts here are the usual assortment of sweet Middle Eastern and Mediterranean offerings, like **Kazan's** variations on baklava and rice pudding. A complimentary sweet after-dinner drink made from pomegranate and banana liqueur, with coffee beans floating on top, is a nice end to a memorable dinner.

NIZAM'S

523 Maple Ave. West (Rt. 123), Vienna, VA (703/938-8948). **Nearest Metro:** Vienna on the Blue/Orange Line. **Hours:** Lunch Tu-F; Dinner Tu-Sat; Sunday Dinner 4:00 pm -10:00 pm; closed Mon. **Credit Cards:** AE, CB, DC, MC, V. **Price:** MODERATE.

Nizam's is one of two consistently good Turkish restaurants in this area, although some of the dishes that get rave reviews are only so-so. The decor is upscale and the waiters wear tuxes. Pretty fancy digs, all in all. But they've saved some of that elegance for the food, as it should be.

First, a small complaint: the dish that has most area critics drooling, the **Doner Kebab**, is okay, but nothing to write home about. The sauce is very heavy, and the meat is sometimes on the tough side. There are better dishes here.

For starters, the assortment platter is a good option for a larger group, where you'll get a nice selection of typical Turkish appetizers. If you order inidvidually, the stuffed grape leaves are particularly good, as is the **Imam Bayildi**, which is one of many worthwhile eggplant dishes on the menu.

For entrées, try the **Famous Turkish Manti**, a plate of delicious small pasta shells stuffed with spiced lean ground beef, served in a garlic-yogurt sauce. The whole thing is topped with real tomato sauce. If you like eggplant, try the **Musakka** (yes, it's just like the Greek *moussaka*, but there's no sense in choosing sides here on the all-important issue of who thought the darn thing up first; the two communities have plenty of other good stuff to fight about). It's one of the best eggplant dishes I've ever had, with ground sirloin and béchamel sauce served over rice pilaf.

The shish kebab dishes are also quite good; my favorites are the **Tavuk Shish Kebab** (marinated chunks of chicken breast, on skewers with onions, tomatoes, and green peppers, served over rice pilaf) and **Kuzu Shish Kebab,** pretty much the same thing except with lamb. The **Karisik Izgara**, a mixed grill of beef and lamb served with rice pilaf, is a good choice if you're feeling the need to fill up on some red meat.

You don't have to be too adventurous to try one of the Turkish wines here; they're a nice complement to your meal. Desserts are standard fare. For an elegant Turkish meal that usually sizzles, try **Nizam's**.

THE BEST VALUES

Abi - Salvadoran
Appetizer Plus - Japanese
Bangkok Vientiane - Laotian/Thai
Bombay Bistro - Indian
Cactus Cantina - Mexican/Tex-Mex
Café Asia - Pan-Asian
CaféDalat - Vietnamese
El Pollo Rico - Peruvian
Haandi - Indian
I Matti - Italian
Jaleo - Spanish
La Cantanita - Cuban
Nam's - Vietnamese
The Chicken Place - Peruvian

GENERAL INDEX

LOCATION INDEX

District of Columbia

FROM THE AUTHOR

You know my picks for Washington's ethnic dining scene, but I'd like to hear yours. Send me your top three choices, or more if you care to, so I can continue to expand and improve this book. And if you disagree with one of my choices, I'd like to hear that too. The address is listed below.

FROM THE PUBLISHER

Our goal is to provide you with a guide book that is second to none. Please bear in mind, however, that things change: phone numbers, prices, addresses, quality of food served, value, etc. Should you come across any new information, we'd appreciate hearing from you. No item is too small for us, so if you have any recommendations or suggested changes, please write. The address is:

Jonathan Stein
c/o Open Road Publishing
P.O. Box 11249
Cleveland Park Station
Washington, DC 20008

YOUR PASSPORT TO GREAT TRAVEL! FROM OPEN ROAD PUBLISHING

THE CLASSIC CENTRAL AMERICA GUIDES

COSTA RICA GUIDE by Paul Glassman, 5th Ed. Glassman's classic travel guide to Costa Rica remains the standard against which all others must be judged. Discover great accommodations, reliable restaurants, pristine beaches, and incredible diving, fishing, and other water sports. Revised and updated. **$14.95**

BELIZE GUIDE by Paul Glassman, 6th Ed. This guide has quickly become the book of choice for Belize travelers. Perhaps the finest spot for Caribbean scuba diving and sport fishing, Belize's picture-perfect palm trees, Mayan ruins, tropical forests, uncrowded beaches, and fantastic water sports have made it one of the most popular Caribbean travel destinations. Revised and updated. **$13.95**

HONDURAS GUIDE by Paul Glassman, 2nd Ed. Paul Glassman's superior series of Central America travel guides continues with the revised edition of his fascinating look at Honduras and the Bay Islands. **$13.95**

GUATEMALA GUIDE by Paul Glassman, 8th Ed. Glassman's first travel guide to Central America, it remains the single best source for visiting Guatemala. **$16.95**

OTHER TITLES OF INTEREST

AMERICA'S MOST CHARMING TOWNS & VILLAGES by Larry Brown. The book everyone's talking about! Larry Brown shows you the 200 most charming and quaint towns in America - all 50 states included. Fun coverage on each town includes local sights, interesting historical notes, and includes information on where to stay and eat. **$14.95**

CHINA GUIDE by Ruth Lor Malloy, 8th Ed. The first guide to modern China and still the best, Malloy has shown you the real China since 1975, now with new sections on Beijing, Shanghai, Xian, Guangzhou, Nanking, and other top Western destinations, plus detailed information on hundreds of distant areas, language tips, travel planning advice, and much more. **$17.95**

DISNEYWORLD AND ORLANDO'S THEME PARKS: THE COMPLETE GUIDE by Jay Fenster. *The* complete guide to Disneyworld and all of Orlando's theme parks (including Sea World, MGM Studios, Busch Gardens, Church Street Station, Spaceport USA, and more), shows you every attraction, ride, show, shop, and nightclub they contain. Includes 64 money-savings tips for hotel, airfare, restaurant, attractions, and ride discounts. **$12.95**

Ask for Open Road's travel books from your favorite bookstore, or order direct. (Please enclose $3.00 for the first book, and $1.00 for each book thereafter for postage and handling). **Discounts available for special order bulk purchases.**

<u>ORDER FROM:</u> **OPEN ROAD PUBLISHING**
P.O. Box 11249, Cleveland Park Station, Washington, D.C. 20008